READING COMPREHENSION SERIES

SWELLS AND SHELLS

Martha K. Resnick

Carolyn J. Hyatt

Sylvia E. Freiman

STECK-VAUGHN
COMPANY
ELEMENTARY · SECONDARY · ADULT · LIBRARY

About the Authors

MARTHA K. RESNICK is an experienced elementary teacher, formerly a Reading Resource Teacher with the Baltimore City Schools. She has served as a cooperative practice teacher, training student teachers from many colleges. Mrs. Resnick received her master's degree in education at Loyola College.

CAROLYN J. HYATT has taught elementary, secondary, and adult education classes. She was formerly a Senior Teacher with the Baltimore City Schools. Mrs. Hyatt received her master's degree in education at Loyola College.

SYLVIA E. FREIMAN has taught primary and upper elementary grades. She has conducted teacher in-service classes, supervised student teachers, and participated in curriculum planning. Mrs. Freiman received her master's degree in education at Johns Hopkins University.

Reading Comprehension Series

Wags & Tags

Claws & Paws

Gills & Bills

Manes & Reins

Bones & Stones

Swells & Shells

Heights & Flights

Trails & Dales

Acknowledgments

Illustrated by Rosemarie Fox-Hicks, Ray Burns, and David Cunningham

Cover design Linda Adkins Design

Cover photograph © TSW/Click-Chicago

All Photographs used with permission. Page 74, © James P. Rowan; Page 78, © Anthony Mercieca/ Root Resources; Page 79, © James H. Carmichael, Jr.; Page 87 (top), © James H. Carmichael, Jr.; Page 87 (bottom), © J. C. Allen/Hillstrom Stock Photo; Page 88, © Stan Osolinski/Root Resources

ISBN 0-8114-1349-7

12 13 14 PO 04 03 02 01

Contents

iv

Winnie and Ben Dorn hated living in Oceanside. They were always getting picked on by the other kids. It was because of the house into which they had just moved.

The children's father had lost his job in the big city where the Dorns had always lived. After a long search, Dad found a new job. The children's excitement over the good news turned to shock when they found out they would have to move to Oceanside, a very small town close to the seashore.

Winnie and Ben were upset. They could not give up their friends, their wonderful school, the library that had everything, and the sports they enjoyed!

Then their mother found an excellent job in Oceanside, too. The Dorns had no choice. They had to move!

Mrs. Dorn tried to cheer up the children. "Guess what?" she said. "We found a big, beautiful house to rent. It's much bigger than the one we live in now. It's well-kept, newly-painted, and the rent is very cheap!"

Ben groaned. At the age of eleven, he knew when he was beaten. Cheap rent! There was no way his parents could turn down cheap rent.

Winnie was nine. She did not know when to give up. "I despise the ocean," she exclaimed. "I'm scared of those waves. The first time we went to Oceanside, I cut my foot on a broken shell on the sand. The sea gulls are loud and messy. I won't go!"

"None of us <u>wants</u> to move, Winnie, but we must," said Dad.

So here the Dorns were, stuck in a tiny village without shopping malls, movies, or all the places for sports and fun they had in the big city. To make things worse, Winnie and Ben had to face a lot of teasing about their house.

It was called the Old Pinkney House. Everyone thought the house was unlucky because in 1885 the whole family that lived there had disappeared. They were never seen or heard from again. Then in 1890, someone searching for clues to the Pinkneys' disappearance also disappeared. From then on, only people new to Oceanside ever lived in the Pinkney house at 743 Wendell Street.

"That's why the rent is so cheap!" teased Amy Smith after school one day. "The owner wants to be sure the rent is paid before you disappear."

"Ha! Ha!" laughed Mamie James. "No use being friends with you two. As soon as I start liking you, you'll disappear."

Every week Don Aster said to Ben, "Don't waste time studying for the math test. You may go up in a puff of smoke before Friday."

The children complained to their parents, but got nowhere.

"Look what a nice place we're getting for next to nothing," said Dad.

Mom added her voice. "Even when we had better jobs and made more money, we never had a house this big or this beautiful. I am very happy here!"

That left Ben and Winnie silent. Knowing how hard their parents worked, they could never complain again.

They could worry about their parents, though, and they did. Mr. and Mrs. Dorn worked long hours and got home late. The children did not voice their fears to each other, but both were afraid that one evening their mother and father would not be home at all because they had disappeared.

"It's up to us to find out what happened to the Pinkneys," Ben told Winnie. That Saturday, they went to see Mr. Jay, the owner of the Oceanside newspaper. Mr. Jay got out copies of the old papers from 1885. The children read the strange story of the Pinkneys' disappearance.

The men of the Pinkney family and many other men from Oceanside had been sailors. Many of the sailors were also smugglers, who used their boats to bring in goods from other places without paying taxes on the goods.

It was believed, the newspaper said, that the Pinkneys were telling the police about what the smugglers were doing. The smugglers had promised to get even with the Pinkneys. Shortly after that, the whole Pinkney family had disappeared.

Five years later, in 1890, Zeke Little, the town handyman, told everyone that he knew what had happened to the Pinkneys. "I'm checking it out. By tomorrow I'll know for sure," said Zeke.

But when "tomorrow" came, strangely enough, Zeke was gone. He, too, had disappeared and was never seen again.

Mr. Jay told the children, "People have always said that the smugglers hid a wonderful treasure somewhere on Wendell Street. Many strangers have come searching for it, but nothing has ever been found. I think that the Pinkneys took the treasure with them when they left town."

1. What kind of story is this?
   a. a funny story
   b. a story to teach people how to work
   c. a story to teach people a lesson
   d. a story about strange happenings

2. What is the difference in the children's ages?
   a. Ben is two years younger.
   b. Ben is two years older.
   c. Winnie is two years older.
   d. Winnie and Ben are twins.

3. Why did Ben and Winnie move to the seashore?
   a. Their grandfather lived there.
   b. They went to learn to swim.
   c. They went to write a mystery story.
   d. Their parents got jobs there.

4. What kind of a house did the family move into?
   a. an old, rundown shack
   b. a new little cottage
   c. a brick house right on the beach
   d. a large, newly-painted house near the ocean

5. Why did the Dorns get the house for so little rent?
   a. It was Mr. Jay's house.
   b. People said bad things about the house.
   c. Mom and Dad had good jobs in the house.
   d. The Pinkneys were moving.

6. What happened first?
   a. The family moved to the house on Wendell Street.
   b. Winnie and Ben got teased after school.
   c. Winnie and Ben searched in old newspapers.
   d. Mr. Dorn found a new job.

7. Why did the smugglers want to get even with the Pinkney family?
   a. The Pinkneys were telling the police about the smuggling.
   b. Mr. Pinkney made more money than the other people.
   c. The Pinkneys tried to sink the smugglers' boats.
   d. Mr. Jay liked the Pinkneys better.

8. What happened in 1890?

   a. The Pinkneys and their pets disappeared.

   b. Mr. Jay started his newspaper.

   c. The Pinkneys built the house on Wendell Street.

   d. Zeke Little disappeared.

9. What is a good name for this story?

   a. Sea Gulls   b. The Unlucky House

   c. Winnie's Cut Foot   d. The New School

B Find the correct word for each meaning. Write the words.

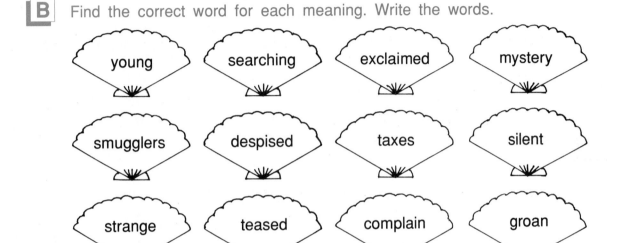

young   searching   exclaimed   mystery

smugglers   despised   taxes   silent

strange   teased   complain   groan

1. something not known   _____

2. not saying a word   _____

3. money paid to a state or country   _____

4. not old   _____

5. people who bring in goods from other
   lands without paying taxes   _____

6. hated   _____

7. looking for   _____

8. made fun of   _____

9. called out   _____

10. a sound of pain   _____

11. unusual or different   _____

C When we read a paragraph or an article, most of the details tell something about a **main idea**. This main idea is the **topic** of the reading matter. The **details** tell more about the main idea.

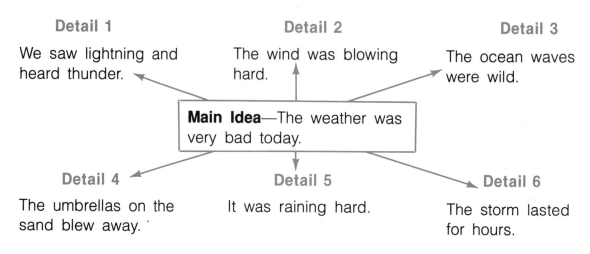

Detail 1

We saw lightning and heard thunder.

Detail 2

The wind was blowing hard.

Detail 3

The ocean waves were wild.

Main Idea—The weather was very bad today.

Detail 4

The umbrellas on the sand blew away.

Detail 5

It was raining hard.

Detail 6

The storm lasted for hours.

Read each group of sentences below carefully. Pick out the main idea in each group. Label it **M.I.** Label each detail **D.**

1.

_____ a. Tiny plants and animals called plankton float near the top.

_____ b. Fishes, squids, octopuses, and whales in the ocean eat plankton.

_____ c. The sea is a home for millions of plants and animals.

_____ d. Animals as different as jellyfish, stingrays, eels, and sharks can be found in oceans.

_____ e. Different kinds of seaweeds grow in the ocean and become food for sea animals.

2.

_____ a. The Pacific is the largest and deepest ocean and covers half the world.

_____ b. The smallest ocean is the cold, icy Arctic Ocean in the far north.

_____ c. The Atlantic Ocean, which reaches from America to Europe and Africa, is the second largest ocean.

_____ d. The third largest ocean, the Indian Ocean, goes down to the cold frozen Antarctic.

_____ e. Salty ocean water covers most of the world.

D Read the following paragraphs. Then read the three topic sentences given. Underline the correct topic sentence for each paragraph.

1. Alligators and crocodiles are members of the reptile class of animals. Turtles are also reptiles. Snakes are members of the same class. Lizards are included, too.

   a. Crocodiles, lizards, and turtles are in the alligator class of animals.
   b. Only snakes and lizards are in the reptile class of animals.
   c. The reptile class has several different animals in it.

2. Reptiles are cold-blooded. This means that their body temperature is the same as the place they are in. In hot deserts, reptiles' body temperature is high. In snow, their temperatures become very low. They go under the ground to keep from freezing.

   a. Reptiles seldom become hot.
   b. This is the way all reptiles are alike.
   c. Cold-blooded animals always have low temperatures.

3. Snakes have no legs, but lizards have four short legs. Lizards have eyelids, though snakes have none. If you look at a lizard's head, you can see ears. Snakes do not have ears. Most snakes have one lung, but lizards have two lungs.

   a. Lizards and snakes are different from crocodiles.
   b. Snakes do not have eyelids, but most other animals do.
   c. It is not hard to tell the difference between snakes and lizards.

4. The bottom scales of snakes are very smooth, so they can slide easily. Snakes also can swim and climb. They can jump through the air from tree to tree. They can move without using legs.

   a. Snakes are able to move in several ways.
   b. Snakes have no legs, eyelids, or ears.
   c. Snakes can climb trees and leap from tree to tree.

When people read newspapers, first they look at the **headlines**. The headline tells the main idea or the topic of each article. If the headline is interesting, a person will usually read the rest of the article.

Choose the correct headline for each article below. Write the headline above the article.

HEADLINES

Wreckers Uncover 100-Year-Old Fortune

100 Pretzels Bring Medal, Money, and Salty Lips

70-Mile-an-Hour Winds Destroy 100 Homes

100 Furs Disappear Through Hole in Roof

_____

_____

1. Workers wrecking an old building at 2758 Thorn Avenue uncovered a secret safe early today. The safe was hidden in an old chimney. When opened, the safe was found to hold a small jar filled with gold coins dating from 1840 to 1848. The jar was wrapped in a newspaper with the date of August 20, 1883. It is thought that the person who hid this treasure forgot about it.

_____

_____

2. A sudden windstorm caused thousands of dollars of damage in Oaktown late yesterday afternoon. Seventy-mile-an-hour winds, with hail and strong rains, ripped the roofs off more than 200 homes. About half of these buildings were destroyed.

_____

_____

3. Dorothy Jean West, age 10, of 98 Daddodil Court was the winner of the annual pretzel-eating contest. Miss West gobbled down 100 of the salty goodies in 40 minutes. The runner-up was Alfred Gray, who ate 99 pretzels. Dorothy Jean's prizes were a medal and a check for $25.

Write your own headline and a short story to go with it below.

_____

_____

_____

_____

_____

_____

_____

F Story 1 had several **expressions** in which the words did not mean exactly what they said. These expressions are used often and people know what they mean. Here are examples:

a. It is time to take a break. This means it is time to rest.

b. It took a long time, but then Winnie saw the light.
   This means that at last Winnie understood.

Here are the **expressions** from Story 1. Write the letter of each meaning next to each expression.

_____ 1. The smugglers want to get even.

_____ 2. The other children picked on Ben.

_____ 3. The rent the Dorns had to pay was next to nothing.

_____ 4. Winnie was left on her own after school every day.

_____ 5. Ben searched for his lost boot, but he got nowhere.

_____ 6. Mother added her voice.

_____ 7. Zeke checked out a hiding place.

_____ 8. The children did not voice their fears.

_____ 9. There was no way his parents could turn that down.

_____ 10. Winnie did not know when to give in.

Meanings

a. very little
b. looked into
c. get back at
d. by herself
e. part of a body
f. speak about
g. stop fighting it
h. teased and made fun of
i. did not succeed
j. spoke
k. say "No"

9

"Treasure!" exclaimed Winnie. "If we can find a treasure, we will be able to move back to the city."

Mr. Jay and the children told Mr. and Mrs. Dorn about the treasure. They all decided to search the grounds around 743 Wendell Street. Some of the Dorns' neighbors joined them.

They searched the woods and the grounds near the house. They searched the stone path that went down to a little brook, and they searched the brook.

After they had looked everywhere else, the searchers came to an old well in front of the house. No one used the well now, and there was a heavy wooden cover over it.

Mr. Dorn and two of the neighbors lifted off the cover. Inside they discovered an old water bucket on a chain. Mr. Dorn tested the chain, then had the neighbors lower him into the well. He went all the way to the bottom, but he found nothing.

"That's enough searching for today," said Mr. Dorn. "Thank you all for your help."

Later that evening, Ben whispered to Winnie, "Let's go down to the basement. Maybe there are some old papers there that will help us."

Winnie and Ben were not teased after school any more. They were not around. They were at home, deep in the basement, looking through old books, pictures, and clothes for some clues.

One day Winnie discovered a faded little painting done by Ann Pinkney, aged seven. At the top was a title, "Our New House, 1875."

The house in the painting looked very different from the Dorn's house. There was no big porch, and there were hardly any trees and bushes around it. The brook was there, though, and so was the stone path.

"And here's the well," said Ben, putting his finger on it. "It's at the side of the house."

Suddenly something caught Winnie's eye. "Look! Here is the front of the house," she exclaimed. "The well is on the wrong side!"

The children went outdoors to check. They stood in front of the house. The well their father had searched was on the left and closer to the brook. The well in the painting should have been on their right and near the side of the house. There was no well there. The ground was flat. A huge stone lay there.

"There was a well here," said Winnie. "I know there was. The Pinkneys must have covered it with this big rock."

That night, the Dorns talked about the children's find. Mrs. Dorn said, "Maybe the well ran out of water. The Pinkneys dug a new well and covered up the old one. The smugglers remembered it and used the old dry well to hide some of their smuggled goods."

"That means the Pinkneys were smugglers, too," said Mr. Dorn. "The well was on their land."

The Dorns worked with the Oceanside police and fire departments and their neighbors to uncover the old well and dig it out. Firefighters had the dangerous job of searching the dark hole. At the very bottom, they found some gold coins and a few old paper dollars. They also found two very old notes.

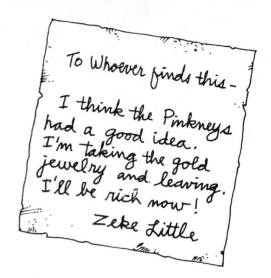

To You Smugglers —
So you want to get even with us! We'll show you! We have taken our part of the money. We are leaving the country. You will never see us again!
John Pinkney

To Whoever finds this —
I think the Pinkneys had a good idea. I'm taking the gold jewelry and leaving. I'll be rich now!
Zeke Little

"That's it," said Ben. "I guess there is no treasure left for us."

"Wait a minute," said one of the firefighters. "These may be worth money." She showed everyone about a dozen tin boxes of different sizes. In each box was a lovely seashell wrapped in silk.

"Those are <u>rare</u> shells!" exclaimed Mr. Jay. "Only a few have been found in the world. They are worth a lot of money."

"The town must decide who owns these things," said a police officer, "but you two kids may get a reward."

"We already have a reward," said Ben. "Everyone here in town worked with us and helped us. It was fun! Now we don't want to go back to the city."

Mrs. Dorn agreed, "Friendship is a treasure."

A Underline the correct answer to each question.

1. What were Ben and Winnie trying to do?
   a. help their parents pay the rent
   b. fix up the house to make it look better
   c. find a treasure
   d. dig a new well to get water

2. What was the children's address?
   a. The story did not say.   b. 743 Wendell Street
   c. 743 Pinkney Street   d. 843 Little Street

3. What is the story mainly about?
   a. how they found out what happened to the Dorns
   b. how they found out what happened to the Pinkneys
   c. how they learned not to care about being teased
   d. how to look up things at the town hall

4. What was the best clue they had?
   a. Mr. Jay's old newspapers   b. the plans at the town hall
   c. a child's picture   d. some old letters

5. Why were the shells thought to be a treasure?
   a. They were in a painting.   b. They were rare.
   c. They were made of gold.   d. They broke into small bits

6. What was the best treasure Winnie and Ben found?
   a. the bucket and the chain   b. some rare gold jewelry
   c. a trip back to their city home   d. happiness in their new home

B Find the correct word for each meaning. Write the words on the lines.

discover	bucket	coins	idea
lowered	neighbor	reward	grounds
basement	enjoyed	faded	rare

1. something given for good work   _____

2. someone who lives near you   _____

3. put it down   _____

4. cents, dimes   _____

5. very seldom found   _____

6. to find out about something   _____

7. underground floor of a house   _____

8. had a good time   _____

9. got lighter   _____

10. the land around a house   _____

11. a thought   _____

13

1. A **fact** is a *true* piece of information. You must be able to prove your facts by showing where you found the information.
2. An **opinion** is what someone *thinks* about a topic. An opinion is not always a fact. This is because people have different opinions about the same topic.

C This is one of the houses the Dorns looked at before they moved to Oceanside. Read what some neighbors said about this old house. Label each statement **fact** or **opinion.**

_____ 1. "The house is haunted."

_____ 2. "That house is run-down."

_____ 3. "That house may give you nightmares."

_____ 4. "The house has a hole in the roof."

_____ 5. "It is dangerous for kids to play on the broken floors."

_____ 6. "I saw a rat run out of the house."

_____ 7. "I think that an old house like that is interesting."

_____ 8. "The owner of the house moved out of the city."

My name is Donna. My friends tell me I'm a good detective. I'm really not, but I do try to think about problems and work them out. You can do it, too.

In my last case, I forgot to use my brain, and the mystery almost didn't get solved. My younger brother, Nicky, sometimes helps with the detective work. That's because I trained him to think, too.

Nicky always walks with his eyes on the ground hoping to find treasures. Mostly, all he comes home with is junk that Mom won't even allow in our apartment.

One morning, Nicky and I were going to the shopping mall. I was admiring an airplane leaving a white trail in the sky. But, as usual, Nicky was crawling around through the bushes.

"This time I've really found something great!" Nicky yelled. "Look, Donna. We need some stones for our window boxes. Now we don't have to buy them."

My brother had discovered a plastic bag filled with pretty colored stones. For a change, Nicky's searching had come up with something useful. We needed some pebbles to put in the bottom of the window boxes. They keep the water away from the roots of flowers so the roots won't rot.

"But these stones are too pretty to hide in the dirt," I said.

"Aw, Donna," said Nicky, "You and Mom never like the good stuff I find. These are mine and I want them to help my plants grow."

At that point, we had reached the walking bridge that led over the busy highway to the huge shopping mall. An older woman with a cane who lived in the next apartment building was behind us.

"Good morning," she said, eyeing Nicky's bag. "What beautiful little pebbles you have there. How would you like to sell them to me? I collect colored stones."

"No, thank you," I answered as we started to walk away.

"Don't rush, children," called the woman. "I need some help across the bridge. It's so far for me to walk."

The woman did look tired. So we each took one of her arms. We slowly walked across the bridge to the mall.

"You are the sweetest youngsters!" the woman said. "How can I thank you? Let me give you $25 as thanks and to buy that worthless stuff in the plastic bag."

"No, ma'am," I said. "We were glad to help you."

Nicky added, "Mom and Dad don't want us to take money for being kind. And I still don't want to sell the pebbles."

So the woman thanked us about a million times. She took our names and address and said she would write a note telling our parents how kind we were. Because we knew she lived close by, we felt safe giving her the information.

When we got home from the mall, we planted the petunias we bought in our flower boxes. We decided to keep four of the beautiful green stones out of the soil because they were so lovely. I put them in my desk.

Two weeks later, something strange occurred. While our family was out, someone broke into our apartment. We could tell because there were muddy footprints everywhere and all the cabinet drawers were open.

"Nothing seems to have been stolen!" exclaimed the police officer. "Did you folks get anything new lately?"

Dad answered, "No we didn't. What could the thief have been looking for?"

The police officer guessed, "I think the thief may have been after money."

"It's lucky," said Mom, "that we don't keep any money in the house."

Later, as Dad and I cleaned up the footprints in the kitchen, an idea stirred in my memory. But I paid no attention because I was boiling mad at the thief.

After the clean-up, we all went outside for some fresh air. I suddenly recalled what had happened out here by the walking bridge.

I dashed back to our apartment. Into my room I flew. I opened my desk drawer. Something was missing! The four green stones were gone! Finally, my brain started to work.

I called the police officer to ask if there were any other crimes in our neighborhood lately. I wasn't surprised to find out that the jewelry store in the shopping mall was robbed at noon a couple of weeks ago. Many valuable rings, bracelets, and necklaces were taken. Precious stones such as emeralds, diamonds, and rubies were also stolen.

In no time police detectives were at our house. They removed our petunias from the window boxes. Then they sifted the soil and found all of Nicky's beautiful pebbles. They were indeed jewels—not worthless stones.

The detectives told us that the robber had been a skinny, short, spry man with a beard. He had put all the jewelry in a briefcase and walked out of the store. Several shoppers had seen him leave by the north entrance of the mall. Then he had disappeared, as if by magic.

My brother said, "The north entrance of the mall is the one closest to our apartment building."

"Good thinking, Nicky!" I exclaimed. I think I can guess what happened."

We took the police detectives across the walking bridge to the mall. We went to the north entrance. Hidden behind a nearby fence were the mall dumpsters.

I explained, "The robber most likely hurried to the fence with his briefcase. See how the thick bushes hide the fence by the dumpsters. Our lively thief climbed over the fence and hid behind the bushes.

"He took out the jewels and threw his briefcase and his beard into the dumpster. He must have had a wig, glasses, a cane, and a blouse hidden there, too. Quickly, the thief became an older woman carrying a bag of jewels.

"From there, it was easy to get to the walking bridge and cross it to our apartments. The bag must have broken. The little package of precious stones dropped out around the bushes. That's where sharp-eyed Nicky discovered it."

From our description of the older woman, it was easy for the police to find the apartment where she lived. Everything she had stolen was in her home. She was arrested and Nicky and I got a reward from the jeweler.

Next time Nicky finds something unusual, we plan to check with the police first thing.

 Read these questions carefully. Then underline the correct answer for each question.

1. What is this story mainly about?
   a. a brother and sister fighting
   b. a young detective solving a problem
   c. how a thief hid jewels, bracelets, and necklaces
   d. how Donna learned to clean the house

2. How long after Nicky found the stones was his home broken into?
   a. two days later   b. a month later
   c. twenty-one days later   d. two weeks later

3. What did the walking bridge cross?
   a. a wide, busy river   b. a body of water
   c. a wide, busy highway   d. some fields

4. Why did Donna and Nicky trust the old woman?
   a. She was an old friend.   b. They trusted everyone.
   c. She was their aunt.   d. She was a neighbor.

5. Why were pebbles put in the bottom of the window boxes?
   a. to hide them from burglars
   b. to keep the fish clean
   c. to keep the roots from rotting
   d. to make the boxes heavy enough

6. Which are not precious jewels?
   a. emeralds   b. diamonds
   c. pebbles   d. rubies

7. When was the jewelry shop robbed?
   a. during the day   b. in the darkness
   c. after midnight   d. The story did not say.

8. Where had the thief hidden the cane, the blouse, and the wig?
   a. on the walking bridge   b. in Donna's bedroom
   c. in the dumpsters   d. in the middle of the mall

9. What was stolen in the break-in?
   a. nothing   b. a television
   c. money   d. something green

10. Why did the woman offer Nicky $25 for the stones in the plastic bag?
    a. She was a rich woman.
    b. She wanted to thank the children.
    c. She knew they were jewels.
    d. She collected stones.

Word Box

lately	concealed	asked	hidden
questioned	happened	occurred	robbers
expensive	burglars	permit	recently
filthy	let	unclean	worthless
			valuable

B To understand sentences we read we must know the meaning of the words in them. To understand a paragraph, we have to know the meaning of each sentence in it.

Read these sentences. Find two words in the word box that mean the same as the underlined word. Write them on the line under the sentence.

1. Dad would not <u>allow</u> the children to speak to strangers.

   _____

2. The green stones were <u>out of sight</u>.

   _____

3. Had there been a robbery <u>a short time before</u>?

   _____

4. The man <u>inquired</u> about renting an apartment.

   _____

5. The <u>thieves</u> escaped with many valuable paintings.

   _____

6. After the cookout, the grill was <u>dirty</u>.

   _____

7. The robbery <u>took place</u> after sunset.

   _____

8. Emeralds are <u>precious</u> stones.

   _____

North

Mall

Freedom Highway

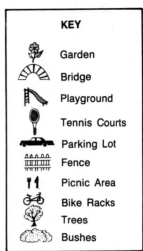

Lee Street

Grant Street

Washington Street

West

East

South

KEY

Garden

Bridge

Playground

Tennis Courts

Parking Lot

Fence

Picnic Area

Bike Racks

Trees

Bushes

C Being able to read maps is an important skill.

1. Maps help you find your way **to** new places.

2. Maps help you find your way **around** in a strange place.

Here is a map of the neighborhood where Donna and Nicky live. There are words on the map to name certain places. The key explains what the pictures or symbols on the map stand for. Study the map. Then underline the correct answer for each question.

1. Donna lives on the street with two apartment houses. What street is it?

   a. Lee Street   b. Washington Street   c. Freedom Highway

2. Which is on Grant Street?

   a. the pool   b. the parking lot   c. the playground

3. Where is Lee Street?

   a. south of Freedom Highway

   b. north of Freedom Highway

   c. by the picnic area

4. Where is the bridge?

   a. across Freedom Highway

   b. across Grant Street

   c. across from the swimming pool

5. Where is the playground?

   a. south of the picnic area   b. east of the pool   c. north of the bike racks

6. What is on Washington Street?

   a. the bridge   b. the picnic area   c. the playground

"This is not my idea of fun," grumbled Kim.

It was a chilly evening in February. Kim Watts was talking to her twin brother Neil. They were working in their father's antique store. Mr. Watts had needed their help to unpack a huge box.

Their father said, "I'm sorry, children. The box was delivered at closing time. It must be unpacked in time for the sale tomorrow."

At last the box was open. Mr. Watts carefully lifted the soft packing. It had protected the antiques on their long trip to his shop. Antiques are old things that were used by people long ago. Mr. Watts sold antiques in his shop.

The twins were not always interested in old plates, paintings, and fans. They disliked having to be so careful about handling them. But they knew it was important not to crack or break the valuable objects.

"This time we have some china dogs," announced Mr. Watts. He unwrapped one.

"It's pretty," said the twins together.

Quickly, all three unpacked more china dogs. Suddenly they stopped! From the bottom of the carton came a strange moan.

"One of the china dogs is barking," said Neil.

Now their father's fingers flew, pulling out everything.

Mr. Watts piled antiques on a table. Soon he tipped the box over on its side. Out of the soft packing material staggered a weak, skinny cat. Every rib in its body showed. It stumbled and fell flat on its face.

"This is strange!" said Mr. Watts. "This shipment took seven weeks to reach here from London! How did this poor cat live so long without food and water?"

The children held the cat. They felt sorry for it. Mr. Watts got the telephone book. He looked through the Yellow Pages. He looked under "Veterinarians." Then he dialed one number after another, trying to find an animal doctor who worked late in the evening. He had no luck.

Kim filled an antique dish with water. Neil put it by the cat's mouth. A swollen, pink tongue tried to lick the water, but the cat was too weak. Neil put some drops of water on his fingers. Slowly the animal licked a few drops.

Kim called Mom at home and asked her to have warm milk ready. Mr. Watts locked the door of the shop. Then they rushed to the car with the cat. On their way home, they passed an open food store.

"Please run in and buy some cans of cat food."
Mr. Watts handed Neil some money.

When they got home, they ran into the house. All of them tried to explain about the cat to Mom. She thought of using an eyedropper to feed the animal. From it, she dripped warm milk into the kitty's mouth. Then she put a tiny bit of cat food on its tongue. The cat swallowed it slowly. Neil and Kim cheered.

Dad took an antique basket and filled it with pillows. Neil gently placed the cat in it. The animal soon fell asleep.

The next day, Mrs. Watts told the veterinarian what had happened.

"The cat was in a box of china from England. The carton traveled by ship across the Atlantic Ocean. In this country, the carton was loaded onto a truck. The truck drove over a large part of the United States to our shop here in Texas. The whole trip took seven weeks."

"That's over 5,000 miles! And all that time without food or water!" exclaimed the doctor. "It's a miracle that the poor thing survived!"

That was how the cat got his new name—Miracle.

 With the doctor's medicine and much loving care, Miracle began to recover. His ribs no longer stuck out. His fur was shiny and smooth. A month later, the little, skinny thing had turned into a large, handsome cat. Miracle was loved by everyone he met.

Soon Miracle was a spoiled animal. He didn't like to stay alone. One day, when the twins were in school and their parents were at work, Miracle sneaked out of the house. Somehow he found his way downtown to the antique shop. Mr. Watts found him lying quietly on the shelf with the china dogs. After that, Miracle went with Mr. Watts to the shop every day.

"Miracle is more careful around the antiques than the twins are," said Mr. Watts. "Why, he's never chipped a thing."

In August, Mr. Watts flew to London to buy more antiques for his shop. After picking out the things he wanted, he started to pay for them. As a joke he said, "You never charged us for that wonderful cat. We like him better than *all* the china dogs put together."

The Englishman, Mr. Lake, looked puzzled. When Mr. Watts explained, Mr. Lake's mouth opened in amazement.

"It must be our company cat, Lucky!" he exclaimed. "We have searched everywhere. We advertised in the papers and offered a reward. Everyone here misses him!"

When Mr. Watts returned home, he had a letter for the twins.

> 23 Pear Street
> London, England
> 10 August 1989
>
> Dear Kim and Neil,
>
> Thank you for taking such good care of our favorite cat. We miss Lucky very much. If you can bring yourselves to part with him, we will give you a free trip to London to bring Lucky back. Once you are here, we would like you to be our guests for two weeks.
>
> Since you saved Lucky's life, he is partly yours. You must decide whether to keep him or bring him back to us in England.
>
> Thank you very much.
>
> Sincerely,
> Alexander Lake

What would you do?

 Read these questions carefully. Then underline the correct answer for each question.

1. What happened first in the story?

   a. A carton arrived from London.

   b. Mr. Watts phoned veterinarians.

   c. Mother used an eyedropper to feed the cat.

   d. Neil bought cat food.

2. What happened last in the story?

   a. Miracle went to the antique shop.

   b. They heard a meow.

   c. The twins got a letter from England.

   d. Lucky got lost.

3. When did Mr. Watts and the twins find Miracle?

   a. early in the day

   b. late in the day

   c. at noon

   d. about midnight

4. What is a *miracle*?

   a. a strange, terrible happening

   b. a long flight across the ocean

   c. a journey without food

   d. a strange, wonderful happening

5. Why do you think the cat was in the carton?

   a. Mr. Lake sent the cat to the United States as a gift.

   b. The packers thought the cat was an antique.

   c. The cat crawled in, and the carton was closed before he could get out.

   d. The cat wanted a vacation in Texas and crawled into the carton.

6. When was the cat found?

   a. in the summer

   b. in the spring

   c. in the autumn

   d. in the winter

7. When did Mr. Watts travel to England?

   a. in the fall

   b. in the summer

   c. in the winter

   d. in the spring

8. What did the story show about the twins?

   a. They were selfish.

   b. They were helpful.

   c. They were careless.

   d. They were mean.

9. Which of these would be an antique?

   a. a coat from last year

   b. a new chair

   c. a picture your mother painted

   d. a table made in 1800

10. How long was Miracle trapped in the carton?

    a. about seventy days

    b. about two weeks

    c. about seven weeks

    d. less than four weeks

11. After Mr. Watts heard the meow, "his fingers flew" as he unpacked the carton. What does that mean?

    a. He waved his hands.

    b. His hands shook with fright.

    c. He worked fast.

    d. His fingers got cut on broken china.

12. In the story, what did Miracle dislike the most?

    a. unpacking the china

    b. traveling to China

    c. taking his medicine

    d. being alone

13. What is this story mainly about?

    a. a helpful veterinarian

    b. a trip on a truck

    c. a journey across the ocean

    d. a cat's strange adventure

14. What will Neil and Kim get if they decide to return the cat to England?

    a. a reward and another cat

    b. a journey to Texas and an orange cat

    c. a free trip to London

    d. nothing at all

15. What did the twins decide to do with Miracle?

    a. keep the cat

    b. return the cat

    c. share the cat

    d. The story does not say.

16. What is the best title for this story?

    a. The China Dogs

    b. Lucky, the Miracle Cat

    c. The Antique Shop

    d. What Are Antiques?

Write the correct word to complete each sentence.

swollen	moan	antiques	veterinarian	sale	skinny	explain
grumble	objects	gentle	valuable	sail	weak	survive

1. An animal doctor is also called a _____.

2. Something that is worth much money is _____.

3. Old objects that were used long ago are called _____.

4. To tell how something works is to _____.

5. Something larger than usual is _____.

6. To complain is to _____.

7. Things are also called _____.

8. To live on is to _____.

9. A quiet groan is a _____.

10. Objects with reduced prices are on _____.

11. Someone who is very thin is _____.

12. Something that is not strong is _____.

13. A thing that is not rough is _____.

C To understand what you read, you must know the meaning of the **details** in the story. The details tell you **where, when, who, what, why,** and **how** about the action. Put all the details together, and you get a better idea of what the author is telling you.

Read the following stories. If you understand the details, you will know what to do with the pictures. Follow the directions carefully.

1. Mr. Watts had five china dogs in the shop window. Three looked just alike, but two others had different details on them. Kim and Neil had a hard time finding the two that did not match. See if you can do it faster. Circle the two dogs that do not match the others.

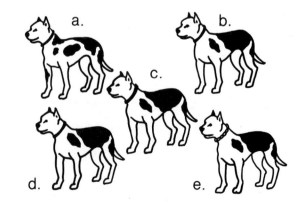

2. The Watts have a nice home. Their wooden house is wide and low. They have trees and bushes around the house, but they have no garage. Mark their home with an **X**.

a.

b.

c.

d.

3. One day Neil and Kim saw this sign in the window of the antique shop. Write complete sentences to answer these questions about the sign.

FREE SHOW!   BIG SALE!

ANTIQUE FAIR

Friday, November 3
8:00–10:00 P.M.

HARBOR HALL
123 Park Street
Marble City

a. How much does it cost to see the show?

_____

b. Where will the antique fair be held?

_____

c. When will the fair be held?

_____

d. What can people do at the fair?

_____

4. Neil and Kim just got two books at the library. They are written by their favorite writers. They know that one book will make them laugh. The other one will puzzle them. Circle the two books.

THE MYSTERY OF THE ANTIQUE BOX

by ANNA HOODIDIT

a.

The Life of a QUARTERBACK

by Michael Gridiron

b.

FISHING MADE EASY

BY I.M.N. Angler

c.

Two Hundred Old Jokes

by Phil O'Chuckles

d.

ANTIQUE TOYS

BY Susan Young Collector

e.

a. Write the names of the authors of the two books Neil and Kim got from the library.

_____

b. Which book might make them laugh? Write the title.

_____

c. Which book might puzzle them? Write the title.

_____

d. Which books might a sports fan read? Write the titles.

_____

e. Who is the author of a book about old toys?

_____

Read the following story. Notice all the details. Then answer the questions following the story.

As Kim and Neil flew to London, they read a story. It was about a boy named Tom Tyler. About 175 years ago, little Tom Tyler lived on the streets of London. After his parents died, he was left alone. No one fed him. No one took care of him. He slept under bridges or in doorways of old buildings. He wore dirty rags and begged for food.

In those days, there were many homeless children in London. Some stole food and coins. Others lived on scraps or money tossed to them by people passing by.

Tom Tyler was skinny and short for his ten years. When someone threw coins to Tom, the other youngsters easily pushed him aside. If the grocer gave Tom an apple, the larger children grabbed it away from him.

One chilly day, Tom stood near a group of workers. They were tearing down an old house. At last, one worker gave him a piece of bread and some meat. Tom was eager to eat the food. He did not watch his step. He stumbled into a hole in the cellar. Then Tom rolled down a slope and hit an old stone wall.

The food fell out of his hand. Tom searched through the loose dirt for it. How happy he was to find it! As he picked it up, he saw ten strange, round things lying in the dirt.

Tom brushed them off. They were coins. They were very dull and had strange pictures on them.

"Money is money," thought Tom. "I'll spend it." He ran to the baker to buy a sweet bun.

When he paid the woman, she began to shout. "Wait, you little thief! You gave me worthless trash!"

She threw the coins on the floor. With a broom, she started to chase Tom. A man standing nearby picked up the coins and rescued Tom.

"They're coins," panted Tom. "Why can't I spend them?"

The gentleman looked closely. He said, "They're not English money. But they are worth much more. These are antique Roman coins. They are hundreds of years old."

Mr. Eaton, the gentleman, helped Tom find a home. He and Tom sold the coins as antiques. The coins earned Tom so much money that he never had to live in the streets again.

Neil and Kim were glad Tom had found a kind person to help him. Then they thought of Lucky. They were also glad they had been able to rescue the cat.

1. Where did the story take place? _____

2. When did the story take place?

_____

3. Why did Tom live on the streets? _____

_____

4. How did Tom get food?

_____

_____

5. What did Tom find? _____

6. How did Mr. Eaton help Tom? _____

_____

7. Who started to chase Tom with a broom? _____

8. Why was Tom unable to spend the coins? _____

_____

9. How did Tom finally get enough money so he did not have to live in the streets?

_____

10. Why were Neil and Kim going to London?

_____

E Now it is your turn to be a writer. First write three details about Tom Tyler when he lived in the streets. Then write three details about Lucky the cat when he was found in the box. Write your details in complete sentences.

Tom Tyler

_____

_____

_____

_____

_____

Lucky the Cat

_____

_____

_____

_____

_____

F On each line, write the letter of the word on the right that matches the definition on the left.

_____ 1. something to cure sickness   a. rescue

_____ 2. ask to a party   b. animal

_____ 3. to save   c. medicine

_____ 4. a beast   d. eyedropper

_____ 5. a box   e. antiques

_____ 6. A cat's tongue did this.   f. invite

_____ 7. something that lets out one   g. swollen
           drip at a time
                                               h. licked

                                               i. carton

33

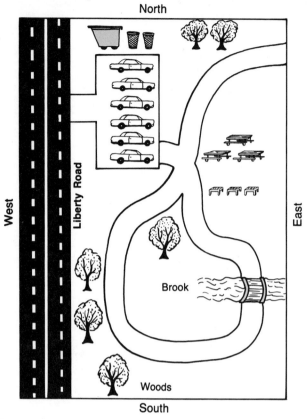

A Study the map above. Then answer the questions.

1. What is south of the dumpster?

_____

2. Is the highway east or west of the picnic area? _____

3. What is the name of the highway? _____

4. Is the brook north or south of the dumpster?

_____

5. What is the nearest thing to the grills?

_____

6. Which is farther away from the eating area, the trash cans or the parking lot?

_____

7. Why are the grills so far away from the woods?

_____

8. By which three ways can you reach the picnic area?

_____

Read the following details. They will tell you where, when, why, how, who, and what. Then you will be able to follow the directions.

1. Molly, Polly, and Dolly were triplets. Mom wanted them to dress exactly alike. Molly and Dolly liked that, but Polly did not. She always wore something extra so her friends could tell which one she was. In this picture you can tell which one is Dolly, too. She has just lost something that the other two still have. Now write the correct name of each triplet under her picture.

_____   _____   _____

2. Read the signs below. Note the details in each. Then answer the questions.

Sign 1   **Sign 2**

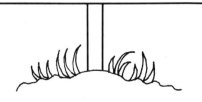

a. Which sign tells about winning something? _____

b. Which sign is a warning? _____

c. Why is Pizza Place closed? _____

d. How long is the contest going to last? _____

e. When will people be able to buy pizzas in Pizza Place again?

_____

f. What must be done to enter the contest? _____

_____

g. How many days will the contest run? _____

h. How can someone get hurt? _____

C Choose the real meaning of each underlined **expression** and write it under the expression.

> **Meanings**
> a. by himself   b. get back at
> c. made fun of   d. understood
> e. all ears   f. say "No"
> g. look into it

1. The girls were <u>picked on</u>.

_____

2. Mark did it <u>on his own</u>.

_____

3. Alice could not <u>turn it down</u>.

_____

4. Let's <u>get even</u>.

_____

5. They <u>saw the light</u>.

_____

6. Please <u>check it out</u>.

_____

D Most details tell something about a main idea. The main idea is also called the **topic.** Details tell about or explain the topic. Read the sentences carefully. Pick out the main idea and label it **M.I.** Label each detail **D.**

1.

_____ a. One of the most important inventions of early people was the wheel.

_____ b. The wheel helped move heavy loads faster.

_____ c. Before the wheel, people had to drag heavy things.

_____ d. The wheel made it possible to take large objects from place to place faster and more easily.

_____ e. People were able to travel longer distances.

2.

_____ a. If a female bird is easily seen and killed by enemies, her eggs will never hatch.

_____ b. When females search for food for baby birds, their colors must blend into the trees and grass.

_____ c. Female birds must blend into the shadows when sitting on nests to hatch eggs.

_____ d. Female birds are not brightly colored like male birds, so they can hide from enemies.

_____ e. Baby birds must depend on their mothers for most of their food.

3.

_____ a. Carrots and potatoes are the roots of plants.

_____ b. Lettuce and spinach are the leaves of plants.

_____ c. Vegetables come from different parts of plants.

_____ d. Celery comes from the stems of plants.

_____ e. When we eat peas, beans, and corn, we eat the seeds of plants.

37

E The topic sentence of a paragraph may be anywhere in the paragraph. Search for the topic sentences in the following paragraphs. Then underline the topic sentence in each.

1. The male ostrich has black feathers on its body. Its small wings and its tail are covered with large, curly, white feathers. These are very lovely. The ostrich's long, thin neck and legs do not have feathers. The skin of the ostrich may be pink or blue. Around its eyes are thick, black eyelashes. What a handsome, unusual bird the male ostrich is.

2. One way monkeys use their paws is to gather and hold their food. Sometimes they use their paws to pick up sticks and banana peels and throw them at other animals. People like to watch a monkey looking through another monkey's fur. The monkey is using its paws to remove dead skin caught in the fur and to look for fleas. The paws make it easy for monkeys to climb trees and swing from branch to branch. Monkeys' paws are useful tools.

3. Nature has prepared the muskrat to spend most of its time in water. The muskrat's fur is warm and waterproof. Its long tail is used for pushing through the water. The webbed feet in the back are good paddles.

F These paragraphs have one or more sentences that do not fit the topic. Draw a line through the sentences that do not refer to the topic sentence.

1. A *gnome* (pronounced nōm) is a creature in fairy tales. Nome is a city in the state of Alaska. The make-believe gnomes were said to look like tiny, old men. They had wrinkled skin and long beards. They were bent and stooped because they worked deep in the earth as miners. Moles also live deep in the earth and dig for food. Gnomes were said to find gold and jewels under the ground which they sometimes gave to kind princes and princesses. Anyone who did not please gnomes was soon repaid with spite and meanness.

2. Birds can travel long distances when they migrate. Bobolinks travel as far as 6,000 miles to spend the winter in South America. The ruby-throated hummingbird travels without stopping 500 miles across the Gulf of Mexico. Columbus traveled many miles on his trips. When the weather becomes warm, the birds fly the same distance to go back north. A round trip for the Arctic tern is 20,000 miles. After their return to the north, robins begin to build nests.

G Melissa and Melvin are from Detroit. They go to Prescott School. Here are some things that their classmates said about them. Some are facts. Some are opinions. Read each statement and label it either **opinion** or **fact.** The first is done for you.

Melissa helped me write a book report.

1. _fact_

Melvin has a hole in his jeans.

2. _____

Melvin is the best-looking boy in Detroit.

3. _____

Melissa won her tennis match.

4. _____

Melissa failed the last math test.

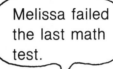

5. _____

Melvin mows the lawn on Saturdays.

6. _____

Melvin is stingy with his baby-sitting money.

7. _____

I think Melissa's tennis shoes are pretty.

8. _____

Melvin tried out for the basketball team.

9. _____

39

As Wayne Hill sat by the pool, his body looked like a question mark. His head was down, and anyone could tell he was sad. He looked like a wilted flower!

"Hey, what's wrong?" asked Rudy Gomez, his friend. "Yesterday you were happy."

Wayne sighed, "Oh, I lost again! That's the fourth time this summer. I was almost last."

Rudy said, "Be like me and don't enter the swimming races. I just swim for exercise."

"That's all right for you," answered Wayne. "Your mother is not a swimming teacher. And your father wasn't the star of his college swimming team."

Rudy nodded. He understood. His mother had been a champion tennis player. So Rudy never played tennis.

Wayne's worst worry was left unspoken. His sister Hannah had a shelf full of diving trophies and medals. She was being trained for the Olympics. People felt sorry for Wayne. They were certain that he was jealous of Hannah.

Grandmother always said, "Practice makes perfect! Try harder. Work at it longer."

Wayne followed her advice. He practiced every day. He worked for hours. His diving was still clumsy. His speed in swimming didn't improve.

As Wayne sat by the pool, the beginners' swimming class started. He saw his little sister Claire in her bright yellow bathing suit. In less than a week, four-year-old Claire had gone from Tadpole class to Minnow class. Now he saw her following the teacher's directions.

Later Claire ran up to Wayne. She was all excited. "I passed the test!" she yelled. "I'm a Sardine now!"

Her teacher followed her. "I've never seen a child learn so quickly!" he said.

"That's wonderful, Claire," praised Wayne, hugging her. "I watched you. You were great!"

"Next, I'll be a Codfish!" exclaimed Claire. "I'll be in the deep water!"

"And I'll be in even deeper trouble," thought Wayne. "My little sister is half-girl, half-fish. And I'm a swimming moose."

The rest of the summer was the same. Wayne's days were spent practicing. Each week he raced. Once he came in third. Everyone was proud. The next week he was last. Meanwhile, Hannah won more medals and trophies. And Claire was now a Dolphin.

Wayne was happy about their success. Still, twice he heard people whisper, "Poor Wayne must be jealous of his sisters."

School began again, but the Hill children still swam on weekends. By now, even Grandmother was telling Wayne to stop entering swimming races. But Wayne wouldn't stop.

"I just have to win once," he said. "Just one time."

In April, several sailing ships from other countries arrived in the city. Everyone was excited. People could visit the harbor and board the ships. Classes from school went to see what life had been like on the old sailing ships.

Wayne's teacher planned a trip to the harbor. How Wayne looked forward to it! He had often sailed on a small

sailboat with his parents. He could hardly wait to see the big sailing ships.

When the day arrived, two classes from Wayne's school visited a ship. It came from Norway. The sailors showed the students how different life had been before engines were invented.

When they left the ship, the teacher counted noses to see if all the students were present.

Wayne and Rudy made sure that they were counted by Mr. Rush. Then they stood watching the smaller boats in the harbor. Many people in the boats were looking up at the sailing ships. Wayne's eye was caught by one houseboat. A baby girl toddled on the deck. Wayne looked for an adult on the boat. But there was no one near the baby.

The little girl got closer to the side. Then she began to climb over the rail.

"Help!" yelled Wayne. "Somebody get the baby!"

No one on the boat had noticed that the baby was on the deck. Wayne's class shouted. As they watched, the child fell into the deep water.

Wayne stopped for a second to kick off his shoes. Then he made one of his clumsy dives. His buddy Rudy was right after him. Wayne was not a fast swimmer, but he was a strong one. He covered the distance without getting tired. But by then, the baby was under the water.

Wayne and Rudy dived under, searching for her. At last, Wayne saw her. She was kicking. As he reached for her, she twisted away. With Rudy's help, Wayne pulled her to the surface. She was choking and struggling to breathe.

All Wayne's months of practice really helped now. He held her and swam to the dock. Rudy had to help hold her part of the time. But Wayne's strong strokes kept them going. When they reached safety, some people pulled them up on the dock. Cheers sounded as the two boys lay panting there.

"It's good that you kept on practicing, Wayne!" exclaimed his father. "There are more reasons to swim than just to win races!"

"You're right, Dad," said Wayne. "I think I'll sign up for the water safety class so I can be a lifeguard."

Young Heroes: Two Boys Save Baby

Wayne Hill and Rudy Gomez are the heroes of Port City. They rescued a child who had fallen from a houseboat. Denise Bell, 2, had gone on the deck as her parents were trying to dock their boat. This took all their attention because the harbor was crowded with traffic around the sailing ships.

When questioned, Wayne told the news reporters that no one else had noticed little Denise, so he dived in to rescue her. Rudy added, "Mr. Rush made me Wayne's buddy. Wherever he went, I had to go. He saved the baby, and I saved him!"

Port City is proud of (continued, page 3)

A Circle the correct answer for each question.

1. To what is Wayne compared in the beginning of the story?

a.   b. 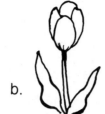   c.    d.

2. What does "Mr. Rush was counting noses" mean?

   a. He was making sure that each child had a nose.

   b. He was making sure that no students were missing.

   c. He was making sure that all noses were pointing in the same direction.

   d. He was counting all the people getting on ships.

3. What is this story mainly about?

   a. Everyone must win a swimming medal or a trophy.

   b. Everyone can do something well.

   c. A visit to a sailing ship can be very interesting.

   d. Girls learn to swim faster than boys.

4. What was Grandmother's first advice to Wayne?

   a. Keep on practicing.

   b. Take lessons in lifesaving.

   c. Practice tennis harder.

   d. Stay with his class at the harbor.

5. Why did Wayne's teacher take the class to the sailing ships?

   a. to see films about Norway

   b. to learn the language of Norway

   c. to teach students how to sail ships

   d. to learn about life years ago

6. Which class came last in Claire's swimming lessons?

   a. Codfish

   b. Dolphin

   c. Minnow

   d. Tadpole

7. Which class came first in Claire's swimming lessons?

    a. Dolphin

    b. Codfish

    c. Tadpole

    d. Sardine

8. Why didn't Wayne win any races?

    a. He did not practice enough.

    b. He raced against better swimmers.

    c. He did not try hard enough.

    d. He was afraid of water.

9. What do you think Wayne will do about his swimming after rescuing Denise?

    a. He will return to the Minnow class and learn to swim again.

    b. He will stop entering races.

    c. He will never swim again.

    d. He will teach others how to win swimming races.

10. Which of these phrases is the best meaning for the word *practice*?

    a. to do over again until you win a contest

    b. to finish the job

    c. always to be perfect at something

    d. to do over and over and over again

11. What lesson did Wayne learn?

    a. Winning is not everything.

    b. Never cry over spilled milk.

    c. His parents did not want him to swim anymore.

    d. It is bad to be jealous of others.

12. How did swimming practice help Wayne?

    a. It helped him to win swimming and diving contests.

    b. It helped him to win medals and trophies for diving.

    c. It made him strong enough to save a drowning child.

    d. It helped him make friends with Rudy.

B What class are you in? Are you a Tadpole, a Sardine, or a Dolphin? For the words in the list below, find **synonyms** (words that mean the same) in the word box. Then write the synonyms next to the words. Check with your teacher. See how many answers you got right. Then look up your score on the scale.

┌─────────────────── **Word Box** ───────────────────┐

rescue   forward   prize
surface   champion   question
search   port   arrive
struggle   tulip   pant

└──┘

1. ahead _____   2. top of water _____

3. harbor _____   4. fight for _____

5. trophy _____   6. get there _____

7. save _____   8. ask _____

9. hunt _____   10. breathe hard _____

SCORES

Answers correct	Class
2	Tadpole
4	Minnow
6	Sardine
8	Codfish
10	Dolphin

Choose the word that best describes each picture. Circle that word.

1.

distance
struggle
attention

2.

struggle
success
advice

3.

exercises
advises
trophies

4.

wilting
exercising
advising

D The **topic sentence** of a paragraph is not always the first sentence. It can be anywhere in the paragraph. Read the following paragraphs. Then find the topic sentence and underline it.

1. Rita Chapa practices at the indoor pool every day after school. She reads books about swimming to improve her strokes. For two years, she has won the city backstroke championship. In races, her team has always finished in first place. <u>Rita is the best swimmer on the team.</u>

2. The Greeks and Romans taught their children to swim early in life. The sport helped them to develop strong, healthy bodies. <u>These ancient people believed that swimming was a very important exercise.</u> Being able to do so prepared the soldiers for land and sea battles.

3. During the Middle Ages, people in Europe were afraid to swim. It was said that going into the water helped spread sicknesses. People seldom took baths either. It was not until 1850 that people found that they could put themselves in water without becoming ill.

4. Because he had lost his math homework, Rudy was kept after school. That made him an hour late for swimming practice. By the time Rudy arrived at the pool, his friend Wayne had gone home.
    "This is certainly not my lucky day!" exclaimed Rudy.
    Just as he said that, he caught his favorite T-shirt on a nail sticking out of the fence. His shirt tore on the nail.

5. Houseboats are floating houses. Unlike other boats, houseboats have flat bottoms. To give enough living space, they have to be wider than other boats. Because of that, they aren't as safe in the water as regular boats are. Houseboats are much slower. They are more difficult to steer, so it takes longer to get them away from dangerous places. Houseboats should always stay in safe, calm waters. <u>These are the main differences between houseboats and other types of boats.</u>

E Now it is your turn to be the writer. Below are three topic sentences. Write four details for each topic sentence. Remember, all the details must refer to the topic sentence.

1. Yesterday was not my lucky day.

_____

_____

_____

_____

2. Now I use the water safety rules every time I go swimming.

_____

_____

_____

_____

_____

3. I'll never forget my first day in swimming class.

_____

_____

_____

_____

_____

F The following paragraphs have one or more sentences that do not fit the topic. Draw a line through any sentence that does not refer to the topic sentence.

1. Heroes are not always people. Sometimes animals can be heroes. A woman fell from a boat into deep water. The woman teaches in my school. While she was trying to swim back to the boat, her leg began to hurt badly. She started to sink. Suddenly a dolphin appeared. It kept her at the top of the water. A dolphin is not really a fish. With its bottle-nose it pushed her along to land.

2. It is not necessary to be a champion to enjoy sports. People swim, bowl, dive, run, jog, play ball, and ride bikes just for fun. People like to go to the library. Strong, healthy athletes stay in shape and feel better. Some people have trouble singing. Girls and boys who play on teams learn that it is okay to win or lose. Just enjoying sports for fun gives people exercise and a good feeling about themselves.

Mrs. Haywire was puzzled. She and Mr. Haywire just did not know what to give Paula for a present. She did not want a bike or skates or a camera. But two weeks before Paula's birthday, Mrs. Haywire overheard her daughter speaking to her friend Alice.

Paula said, "For my birthday, I wish someone would get me a puffin!"

Mrs. Haywire giggled to herself. A puffin! Now she could make Paula happy. She would surprise Paula with the very thing she wanted.

There was only one problem. What in the world was a puffin?

Mrs. Haywire knew Paula had the appetite of a starving shark. She always gobbled up everything on her plate. A puffin was probably some kind of a dessert. Mrs. Haywire was a wonderful cook. She decided to make a puffin for Paula.

Off went Mrs. Haywire to the store;
She walked through the desserts in row number four.
She saw boxes and bags back by the door
Piled up to the ceiling and down to the floor.

A pancake, a brownie, a cookie, a muffin,
But nothing to help her bake a puffin.
She went to the manager to inquire why.
He smiled, "A puffin you just can't buy."

Mrs. Haywire asked where she should go;
The manager told her, "I do not know."
So Mrs. Haywire went from place to place,
And everyone showed her a puzzled face.

"Where do I look for a puffin?" was her sad cry.
Someone said, "Why not give the dictionary a try?"

A Read the list below to learn how to use a dictionary.

USING THE DICTIONARY

1. To help you find words easily and quickly, the words in a dictionary are arranged in **alphabetical order**.

2. The words in alphabetical order are in darker print. They are called **entry words**.

3. At the top of each page are two **guide words**. The first guide word is the first entry word on the page. The second guide word is the last entry word on the page.

4. All the entry words on the page, arranged in alphabetical order, come between the two guide words.

5. The entry words are broken into **syllables**. A syllable is a part of a word. eg: pud•dle

6. Beside each entry word is its **pronunciation**. The pronunciation shows you how to say the word correctly. eg: (pud ′əl)

Look at the guide words and page numbers below. Which page does Mrs. Haywire need to use to find out what a *puffin* is? Mrs. Haywire

needs page ———.

pull	**108**	**punch**
prove	**101**	**prune**

pudding	**106**	**pug**
punish	**109**	**put**

Find *puffin* on this dictionary page below. Help Mrs. Haywire learn what a puffin is.

pud•dle (pud′ əl): **1** *n* : a small pool of dirty water **2** *n* : a small pool of any liquid
puff (puf) **1** *v*: to breathe quickly **2** *n* : a short, quick blast
puf•fin (puf′ ĭn) *n* : short-necked northern sea bird
pull (pull) *v* : to move toward oneself
punch (punch) **1** *v* : to poke **2** *v* : to hit **3** *n* : a quick blow with the fist **4** *v* : to make a hole in

What did Mrs. Haywire learn that a puffin is?

"A puffin's a bird that lives by the sea.
No wonder those people looked strangely at me!
Next time I hear a word that I don't know,
Straight to the dictionary I will go!"

Underline the correct answer for each question.

1. Where did Mrs. Haywire go first to get a puffin?
   a. to the dictionary
   b. to the zoo
   c. to the food store
   d. to Alice's house

2. What is the main idea of this story?
   a. how to pick out a good birthday present
   b. a trip to the grocery store
   c. how to learn from pictures
   d. why and how to use a dictionary

3. What is the best title for this story?
   a. Rhymes Are Fun
   b. Alice and Paula Plan a Party
   c. Mrs. Haywire Learns Something
   d. Mrs. Haywire, a Good Cook

4. Why did Mrs. Haywire use the dictionary?
   a. She wanted to know the meaning of a word.
   b. She wanted to find out where Alice lived.
   c. She was looking for information on how to bake a puffin.
   d. It was the only book in the house.

5. What is a *puffin*?
   a. a small bird that sings sweetly
   b. a large, fat bird that lives in the desert
   c. a bird that lives near the ocean
   d. a kind of peacock

6. How many syllables are in the word *puffin*?
   a. four   b. two
   c. three   d. one

7. What name is given to each word that is explained in the dictionary?
   a. contest
   b. entry word
   c. guide word
   d. syllable

8. What are guide words?
   a. all the entry words on the page
   b. the first and last entry words on the page
   c. all the meanings on the page
   d. the last entry word on each page

9. Which of these would be a dessert?
   a. cream puff
   b. puffin
   c. cherry tree
   d. roasted chicken

10. What does *to inquire* mean?
    a. explain about
    b. ask about
    c. shout about
    d. roast and cook

C Be like Mrs. Haywire. Use the following dictionary page to answer the questions.

sa•ble (sā′bəl) *n* : a small animal valued for its dark, glossy fur
safe (sāf) **1** *adj* : free from danger **2** *n*: a place for keeping valuable things
sail (sāl) **1** *n*: a piece of cloth attached to a ship's mast so the wind will move the ship **2** *v* : to move on water
sale (sāl) **1** *n* : selling something for money **2** *n* : selling at lower prices than usual
salm•on (sam′ ən) *n* : a large, yellowish-pink fish with silvery scales
sand•pa•per (sànd pa pər) **1** *n* : paper with a layer of sand glued on it **2** *v* : to smooth with this paper
saw (sô) **1** *n* : a tool for cutting that has a thin blade and sharp teeth on the edge **2** *v* : to cut with such a tool
scale (skal) **1** *n* : the size of something **2** *n* : a machine for weighing **3** *n* : plate covering fish and some animals

1. How many meanings are given for the word *saw*?_____

2. How many syllables are in the word *sandpaper*?_____

3. A salmon is a_____

_____

4. What is the meaning of *scale* that fits the sentence below?

Mother removed the **scales** from the fish she caught.

_____

5. The fur of which animal is used to make coats? _____

6. Which word and meaning best describe the picture below?

_____

7. Which meaning of the word *sail* is used in this sentence:

The girl raised the **sail** on the boat.

_____

_____

8. Which two words are pronounced the same way?

_____

9. What would you use to see how much you weigh?

_____

10. What might a carpenter use to smooth a piece of wood?

_____

D Be a fortune teller! Predict what will happen to Paula on her birthday. To **predict** means **to tell what will happen in the future.** Some fortune tellers claim to be able to look into the future. Read the following sentences. Make a ✓ by the ones that you can safely predict **might** happen on Paula's birthday. Make an **X** by the ones that could not happen.

_____ 1. Paula's birthday cake will be shaped like a puffin.

_____ 2. Mrs. Haywire will stuff and roast a puffin for Paula's birthday dinner.

_____ 3. Paula will get a present of puffin eggs in a nest. She will sit on the eggs to hatch them.

_____ 4. Alice will come to Paula's party.

_____ 5. Paula will get presents from her parents.

_____ 6. Paula will get a real puffin as a present.

_____ 7. Paula will not get a real puffin as a present.

_____ 8. Puffins like cold weather, so Paula will keep her puffin in the refrigerator.

_____ 9. Paula will keep her puffin in the bathtub with ice cubes around it.

_____ 10. Paula will get a picture of a puffin.

_____ 11. She will get a stuffed toy puffin.

_____ 12. Paula will get a book about puffins.

_____ 13. Mr. Haywire will try to rent a film about puffins to show at Paula's party.

_____ 14. Mrs. Haywire will get Paula a puffin.

_____ 15. Paula's parents will let her keep a family of puffins at home.

Now it is your turn to be a writer. Find the words in the dictionary on page 47. Write a complete sentence for each of the two meanings of these words: scale, saw, and safe.

1. a. _____

_____

b. _____

_____

2. a. _____

_____

b. _____

_____

3. a. _____

_____

b. _____

_____

F Write a word to complete each sentence.

strange	problem	giggle
manager	appetite	inquire

1. The _____ opened the store early.

2. The puffin has a _____ beak.

3. To ask a question is to _____.

4. The deep snow made it a _____ to get to school.

5. The funny story made the kids _____.

7

In 1900, in the small town of Dalton, there were two women with modern ideas. Mrs. Hyde, the mayor's wife, carried on a contest with Mrs. Rush, the banker's wife. They tried to see who could outdo the other in buying new things. Mrs. Rush put in the first telephone in town. Mrs. Hyde got the first upright piano. Mrs. Hyde bought the first box camera. Then the Rushes got the first gramophone, an early record player. The contest between the two women went on.

In April, Mrs. Hyde startled the town by riding down Main Street in an automobile. It was the first seen in Dalton. The horses in the street bucked and kicked and ran away. Mrs. Rush turned emerald green with jealousy. But she was too scared even to think of riding in that noisy monster. What could she buy now to outdo Mrs. Hyde?

She thought for four weeks. Finally she had it! A bathtub with its own water heater was brought into the Rush house. This was a brave thing to do. The newspaper had just printed articles by famous doctors. They informed the people that too much bathing could cause many illnesses.

But Mrs. Rush was firm. The Hydes might ride in style. But her family would be the neatest and cleanest in town.

That was when Lenny Rush's troubles began! Up until then, Saturday night had been the worst time of the week. Then the whole family, even grumbling Grampa, bathed for Sunday. Now, every time Lenny got dirty hanging around the stable, he suffered for it. He was put into the tub and bathed. Once he had to take five baths in one week!

His sister Diana, who was sixteen, complained almost as much as Lenny did. She, too, was tubbed and scrubbed often.

One day in June, Lenny had his fourth bath in four days. Mrs. Rush looked him over.

"Are you sure that ring around your neck is gone?" she asked.

Lenny screamed back,

"Yes, Mom! I'm clean and mean!
My skin's scrubbed raw!
Your bathtub should be against
   the law!"

After that, Father, Grampa, Diana, and Lenny Rush always said that rhyme when being forced into the tub.

Mrs. Hyde had a daughter, Polly, the same age as Diana. Diana was jealous when her friends were always at Polly's house now. They were hoping for rides in the automobile. One day Diana and Lenny sang to their mother,

"Everyone is nice to Polly,
A ride in her auto is quite jolly.
But people look at us with pity
The cleanest ones in the city!
Put wheels on the tub so we can
   ride,
And we'll be as popular as Polly
   Hyde!"

In August, the county judge's family held their yearly watermelon party. All the young folks in town were invited.

They had ice cream, melons, games, and singing. At sunset, scrubbed and sparkling, Diana and Lenny joined their friends. They walked up the hill to the judge's large house.

When Lenny and Diana entered the garden, their friends came to greet them. Lenny saw a crowd of young men by the swing. At parties the older boys always gathered around Elly Morgan. She was the prettiest girl in town.

Suddenly, Elly appeared from the group of boys. Lenny looked at her large, blue eyes and her cloud of wavy hair, as golden as a field of ripe wheat. No one would have ever dreamed that Elly was the poorest, hardest-working girl in town. Her father was dead. Elly, the oldest of five girls, had to work on the farm with her mother. She also had to help raise the younger kids. She was often unable to attend school for days at a time.

Now she pushed her way out of the crowd of admiring boys. She rushed over to Diana and Lenny.

"Diana, you are so lucky!" Elly exclaimed. "Imagine! You can take a bath without boiling water on the kitchen stove. You don't have to mop up the wet floor afterwards!"

"We don't think we're lucky!" complained Diana. "I've been soaked so long that I feel like a wrinkled prune."

"It would be nice for me after working in the fields," sighed Elly. "And it would really help with bathing my two younger sisters."

Then Elly looked at Lenny. Never before had she even noticed him.

"Why, Len!" she cried. "How handsome you look! You're growing up into a very good-looking, young man!"

Lenny saw all the older boys watching him jealously. He put on what he hoped was a charming smile. He said shyly, "Aw-w-w-w!"

"Would you like to come to our house sometime for a bath, Elly?" asked Diana.

After that, Grampa could not believe his eyes when he saw his two grandchildren take baths *every day*. He moaned,

"Look at that! One word from a girl
And Lenny's head is in a whirl!
He'll bathe and soak and clean and scrub
And never again grumble about that tub!"

By then, Mrs. Rush had all that she could stand. She announced in a loud voice,

"Rhymes at breakfast! Rhymes at noon!
I don't like rhymes! Stop it soon!
The next one who dares to say a rhyme,
Will not be eating at suppertime!"

Thanks to the contest between Mrs. Hyde and Mrs. Rush, the whole town started to try new inventions. Dalton soon became known as the cleanest and most modern town around.

 Underline the correct answer for each question.

1. When does this story take place?
   a. in the future
   b. in the past
   c. at this time
   d. twenty years ago

2. How often does the judge's family have the watermelon party?
   a. every six months
   b. every twelve years
   c. every winter
   d. every twelve months

3. Which of these would be the best title for this story?
   a. A Bathtub on Wheels
   b. The Prettiest Girl in Town
   c. The First Horseless Carriage
   d. The Battle of the Bathtub

4. Which of these happened first?

    a. Lenny suddenly liked to take baths.

    b. Mrs. Hyde got the first automobile in town.

    c. Mrs. Rush got the first telephone in town.

    d. Elly admired Lenny.

5. What color was Elly's hair?

    a. black   c. blonde

    b. red   d. gray

6. What happens last?

    a. Laws are passed against bathtubs.

    b. There are fewer bathtubs.

    c. The town tries new inventions.

    d. The Rushes write a poetry book.

7. When did the first automobile appear in Dalton?

    a. spring   c. winter

    b. fall   d. summer

8. Mrs. Hyde and Mrs. Rush always tried to *outdo* one another. What does this mean?

    a. to get something outdoors

    b. to do better than

    c. to show off outdoors

    d. to get something out

9. What is this story mainly about?

    a. how rhymes and poems are written

    b. how the automobile was invented

    c. people trying out new inventions

    d. people trying to invent something new

10. Which of these was a new invention in 1900?

    a. the stove   c. the helicopter

    b. the automobile d. the wheel

11. Why do most people buy new inventions?

    a. to help the inventors

    b. to make work harder

    c. to waste money

    d. to make work easier and faster

12. What would happen to Diana and Lenny if they rhymed again?
    a. They would have to prepare supper.
    b. They would have to wash dishes.
    c. They would miss a meal.
    d. They would have to clean the dirty ring around the tub.

13. Why did Lenny suddenly begin to take more baths?
    a. He liked to swim.
    b. He was turning into a fish.
    c. He wanted to impress Elly.
    d. His grandfather made him.

B Choose a word from the list below to complete each sentence.

monster	upright	emerald
informed	outdo	modern
judge	stable	dirty
mayor	gramophone	banker
suddenly	wrinkled	admire

1. To look at with pleasure is to _____.

2. Something that stands straight is _____.

3. A thing that is new or just invented is _____.

4. A green jewel is an _____.

5. A person who decides what is fair is called a _____.

6. A person who handles money is a _____.

7. A place where horses are kept is a _____.

8. The head of a town or city is the _____.

9. An imaginary and frightening thing is called a _____.

10. An early record player is known as a _____.

11. To do better than is to _____.

12. Something that is not clean is _____.

13. To be told is to be _____.

Follow the directions carefully to answer each question.

1. It took Mrs. Rush four weeks to decide how to outdo Mrs. Hyde. Underline all the answers that mean the same or almost the same as four weeks.

   a. seven days

   b. a year

   c. about a month

   d. twenty-eight days

   e. about two months

   f. a season

2. Before getting the new bathtub, Lenny took a bath every Saturday. How often did Lenny bathe? Underline one answer.

   a. yearly

   b. weekly

   c. monthly

   d. daily

3. After Elly admired Lenny, how often did he bathe? Underline two answers.

   a. monthly

   b. seven days a week

   c. never again

   d. five days a week

   e. daily

   f. once a week

4. Mrs. Hyde got her new box camera in February. What season of the year was it? Underline one answer.

   a. spring

   b. autumn

   c. summer

   d. winter

5. Mrs. Rush got her gramophone a month later. What month was it? Underline one answer.

   a. September

   b. March

   c. June

   d. May

6. The judge's family had a watermelon party every August. What season of the year was it? Underline one answer.

   a. spring

   b. July

   c. summer

   d. fall

7. Elly had to help take some cows to the market. She missed three weeks of school. How many school days did she miss? Underline one answer.

    a. twenty-one

    b. thirty

    c. fourteen

    d. fifteen

8. Grampa was getting ready to go on a trip. He took his bath at sunset. When did he take his bath? Underline one answer.

    a. morning

    b. noon

    c. evening

    d. midnight

9. The train left at dawn. When did the train leave? Underline two answers.

    a. sundown

    b. sunrise

    c. late afternoon

    d. noon

    e. early morning

10. Grampa was seventy years old in 1900. In what year was he born? Underline one answer.

    a. 1829   b. 1830

    c. 1930   d. 1929

11. Grampa came to the prairie in a covered wagon when he was a child. His parents left West Virginia in February and got there in ten months. In which month did they get to the prairie? Underline one answer.

    a. December

    b. February

    c. June

    d. September

12. Grampa waited at the station for thirty minutes. Then the steam engine came puffing in. How long did Grampa wait? Underline one answer.

    a. an hour

    b. two hours

    c. a half-hour

    d. a minute

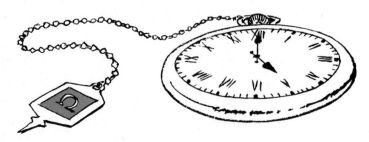

D Choose a word or words from below to complete each sentence. Some words will be used more than once.

one hour	one day
one week	one month
thirty	forty-two days
one minute	thirty-five days
one year	semester
six months	one second

1. Sixty seconds make _____.

2. Twenty-four hours make _____.

3. Three hundred sixty-five days make _____.

4. Sixty minutes are _____.

5. Twelve months are _____.

6. There may be thirty-one days in _____.

7. There may be twenty-eight days in _____.

8. Seven days make _____.

9. A half-year is _____.

10. Six weeks are _____.

11. A half-hour has _____ minutes.

12. A half-minute has _____ seconds.

For a month, Miss Lutz's class had been learning how to use the dictionary to find word meanings. They also searched in the encyclopedia for information. Now an important day had come.

"This is it, class!" exclaimed Miss Lutz. "Each of you will have your own topic. Each of you will be a detective! You must decide where to look for information about your topic. After careful reading, prepare a list of ten interesting facts you have discovered. Every topic will be different. Because of that, you can't work together."

Miss Lutz had a stack of small cards. She walked about the room and gave each student one card face down. When she finished she said, "Get ready, detectives! Get set! Go!"

Every child flipped over the card to see his or her topic. There was not a sound at first. Then some students began to mumble!

"I don't even know what this is!" cried Miguel. "What is a *gauntlet*?"

"That's nothing!" exclaimed Soo-Lin. "I can't even say mine!" She spelled out "l-a-p-i-s l-a-z-u-l-i."

Miss Lutz looked at the puzzled youngsters and smiled. "So what are you going to do about it?" she asked.

Some children went straight to the large dictionary. Others remembered what they were to do with their topics. They went to the set of encyclopedias in the school library.

You can help Miss Lutz's students. See how many questions you can answer about using the encyclopedia.

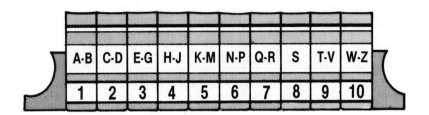

A-B	C-D	E-G	H-J	K-M	N-P	Q-R	S	T-V	W-Z
1	2	3	4	5	6	7	8	9	10

1. Each book in a set of encyclopedias is called a **volume**. How many volumes are in the set above?_____

2. Topics beginning with certain letters can be found in Volume 5. Which beginning letters are found there?_____

3. Which beginning letters are found in Volume 8? _____

4. Which beginning letters are found in Volume 1? _____

5. Which beginning letters are found in the last volume?_____

6. What is the number of the last volume?_____

7. Help Soo-Lin. In which volume would she search for information about *lapis lazuli* ?_____

8. Arthur had to look at his card several times. He had never heard of a *tuatara* . In which volume should Arthur search? _____

9. Marion found her information in Volume 5. Which topic could she have been looking for: *amanita, lepidoptera,* or *gecko?*_____

10. Cecelia was reading Volume 3. Which of these could have been her topic: *simian, jackal,* or *fungi?*_____

11. Miguel's card had the word *gauntlet* . In which volume should he search?_____

12. Chris found *yak* on his card. In which volume should he search?_____

13. Lee found his information in Volume 10. Which topic could he have been looking for: *whirligig, umber,* or *zither?*_____

14. Alex's card had the words *troy weight* . In which two volumes should she search?_____

1	2	3	4	5	6	7	8	9	10	11	12
A-Bo	Br-Du	Ea-Ga	Ge-Hi	Ho-Kn	Ko-Na	Ne-Po	Pu-Rh	Ri-Sa	Sc-Sn	So-Tu	Va-Zy

1. Which volume number must José look in to find facts about

   glockenspiel ? _____

2. What beginning letters are on José's volume? _____

3. Here is Amy Jo's card: whelk . Which volume number should she look in?

   _____

4. What beginning letters are on the volume Amy Jo should look in?

   _____

5. Which volume number must Han look in to find facts about

   Tasman Sea ? _____

6. What beginning letters are on Han's volume? _____

7. Write the number and the beginning letters of the volume you should look in to find each of these topics.

Topic	Number	Letters		Topic	Number	Letters
a. onager	_____	_____		e. oleander	_____	_____
b. gecko	_____	_____		f. narwhal	_____	_____
c. puffin	_____	_____		g. ivory	_____	_____
d. piranha	_____	_____		h. anemone	_____	_____

8. What beginning letters are on the volume that contains periwinkle ?

   _____

68

Underline the correct answer for each question.

1. How are the dictionary and the encyclopedia alike?
   a. They both have many volumes.
   b. They are written in alphabetical order.
   c. The volumes of both are numbered.
   d. They are not alike in any way.

2. How are the encyclopedia and the dictionary different?
   a. Only the encyclopedia has pictures.
   b. Only the dictionary is written in alphabetical order.
   c. The encyclopedia gives more information on each topic.
   d. They are not different in any way.

3. What would *not* be a good use for an encyclopedia?
   a. to find out something new about worms
   b. to learn about a country far away
   c. to find out what the first airplanes looked like
   d. to read today's news

4. What would *not* be a good use for a dictionary?
   a. to find word meanings
   b. to find the spelling of a word
   c. to find out how many syllables are in a word
   d. to study the life of Abraham Lincoln

5. Which of these can you find in a dictionary?
   a. how to say a word
   b. how to fix a broken automobile
   c. the steps in building a log cabin
   d. a road map of your state

6. Which of these can be found in an encyclopedia?
   a. a list of the grocery stores in your hometown
   b. lessons on how to play the piano
   c. information about the weather tomorrow
   d. information about polar bears

7. Under which of these encyclopedia topics would you look to find out who is the home-run champion of the United States?
   a. football   b. baseball
   c. swimming   d. toys

D Pierre is one of the boys in Miss Lutz's class. Here is some information that Pierre found in the encyclopedia about his topic. Read it and answer the questions.

Onager is the name of an animal in the horse family. It is wild and travels in a herd. The onager looks very much like a donkey. In the summer it is dark brown, but in the winter its fur coat turns to yellowish-brown. It has a black stripe down its back. The onager has a mane. At the end of its tail is a tuft of hair.

Herds of onagers can be found on the hot, dry grasslands of central Asia. They are very fast runners. This protects them from their enemies.

1. Is the onager a living thing? _____

2. Are onagers found alone or in groups?_____

3. Where are onagers found? Underline four correct answers.
   a. Africa
   b. South America
   c. Asia
   d. jungles
   e. grasslands
   f. mountains
   g. a dry place
   h. a hot place
   i. a rainy place
   j. a cold place

4. To which family does the onager belong? _____

5. Which animal does the onager look like?_____

6. When is the onager lighter in color? _____

7. What runs down the onager's back? _____

8. How does running fast protect onagers? _____

   _____

9. How many meanings did Pierre find for the word *onager*? Look in your dictionary._____

10. How many meanings did Pierre report on? _____

11. Why do you think the onager changes colors? Underline four correct answers.

    a. for protection from enemies

    b. to look more beautiful

    c. to show it is getting older

    d. so it cannot be seen easily

    e. to match the color of the land

    f. to stay warmer in winter

    g. to be safe from hunters

12. Underline all the facts that are true about what an onager looks like.

    a. has wings

    b. has claws

    c. is four-legged

    d. has a mane on its legs

    e. has a stripe on its chest

    f. has a tuft on its tail

    g. has a stripe on its back

E Now it is your turn to be a writer. Choose one of the topics below. Look up the topic in an encyclopedia. Then write a short paragraph below about what you have learned. Be sure your paragraph has a topic sentence and details that refer to the topic sentence.

condor	Thomas Paine	trilobite
Millard Fillmore	San Marino	Tutankhamen
Geronimo	Socrates	ventriloquism
Milky Way	termites	wombat

_____

_____

_____

_____

_____

_____

A Read the following stories. Notice the details. Then write complete sentences to answer the questions.

1.

Mrs. Jukes saw this ad at 6:00 in the morning. First, she told her friends, Mrs. Frost and Mr. Eisen. Then they all got ready. They left their homes at 8:30. It took Mrs. Jukes sixty minutes to drive to the store. It took Mr. Eisen three-quarters of an hour. It took Mrs. Frost an hour and five minutes.

a. Who got to the store first?

_____

b. Who got there second?

_____

c. Who got the ring?

_____

2. You have heard the story of the tortoise and the hare. The hare was faster, but he stopped for a nap during the race. He lost the race. But he wanted a rematch. The hare and the tortoise raced again. See who won this time. It took the tortoise 70 minutes to finish. It took the hare one hour and ten minutes. This time the hare stopped at the water fountain for a drink.

a. Who won the race?

_____

b. How many minutes did the hare take to finish?

_____

3. The tortoise really thought he was a fast runner. He dared a young snail to race him.

"We'll race to the next state line!" exclaimed the proud tortoise.

"You're on!" said the snail.

The snail reached Kentucky eight weeks later. The tortoise panted over the finish line in sixty-three days.

a. How many days did the snail travel?

_____

b. How many weeks did the tortoise travel?

_____

c. Who got to Kentucky first?

_____

4. On the shelf was a large set of encyclopedias. Each letter was in a separate volume. Every volume had the same number of pages. Two bookworms looked at this set. They were hungry for knowledge.

They decided to see which one could swallow more facts in twenty weeks. Milt started from Volume *A*, and Gil started from Volume *Z*. They ate toward the middle. Exactly twenty weeks later, their friend, Lady Agatha Bookworm, called them out. Milt had chewed his way from *A* through *D*. Gil had eaten his way from *Z* through *V*.

a. How many days did Gil and Milt feast on facts?

_____

b. Who ate through more volumes?

_____

c. How many volumes were eaten through by Gil?

_____

d. How many volumes were eaten through by Milt?

_____

e. If you had to look up information on the following topics, would the volume you need for each be spoiled by worm holes? Write *yes* or *no*.

_____ 1. bobolink

_____ 2. kangaroos

_____ 3. satellites

_____ 4. armadillo

_____ 5. woodpecker

_____ 6. yogurt

_____ 7. United States

5. On February 1, Grace Groundhog woke up in her hole in the ground. She had spent most of the winter sleeping.

"Tomorrow is Groundhog Day," she said to herself. "It's my day to rise and shine. All the reporters and photographers will be out there waiting for me. They want to see if I will see my shadow. If I do, spring will not come for six weeks."

Dawn is a good time for groundhogs to see their shadows. But Grace took a long time getting ready for the photographers. She crawled out from the earth at sunset. The reporters were still waiting. In the light of the setting sun, Grace saw her shadow. It looked slim and lovely. But all her preparations had made her very tired.

"Spring will be late this year!" promised Grace. "I'm going back to sleep."

"Grace is amazing!" all the reporters said.

a. What day is Groundhog Day?

_____

b. What season is it in?

_____

c. When is it a good time for a groundhog to see its shadow?
   Circle one answer.

   sundown   sunrise   Sunday   midnight

d. When did Grace come out? Circle one answer.

   evening   midnight   morning   sunrise

e. In spite of what Grace said, spring arrived at the usual time. When is that? Circle one answer.

   November   January   March   August

B Below is a set of encyclopedias. Study them carefully. Then write complete sentences to answer the questions.

A-Bo	Br-Dy	Ea-Ga	Ge-Hi	Ho-Kn	Ko-Na	Ne-Po	Pr-Rh	Ri-Sa	Sc-Sn	So-Ty	Va-Zy
1	2	3	4	5	6	7	8	9	10	11	12

1. Which volume would have information for Janice about the *paddock*?

   _____

2. What letters are on Volume 3?

   _____

3. Ed searched in Volume 8. Which of these topics did he find there?

rhododendron	polo	radon
clematis	pueblo	roebuck

   _____

4. Natalie was looking in Volume 5. What topics can she find there? Make a ✔ by each one. Put an **X** next to the ones that will not be found there.

   _____ a. hippopotamus   _____ f. hominy

   _____ b. knuckles   _____ g. indigo

   _____ c. krypton   _____ h. homesteader

   _____ d. helmet   _____ i. Kurdistan

   _____ e. jodhpurs   _____ j. hydroponics

5. Some topics contain two or more words. Information might be obtained from more than one volume. Write the numbers of the two volumes in which each of these topics might be found.

   a. Colossus of Rhodes   _____   _____

   b. pampas grass   _____   _____

   c. Oslo Fjord   _____   _____

   d. Mohawk Trail   _____   _____

6. Fred's topic was *pine beetle*. First, he looked for *pine* and found no information in that volume. Then he looked for *beetle* and found no information. Under what other topics might he look? Make a ✔ by two answers.

   _____ a. pesticides   _____ b. insects

   _____ c. leaves   _____ d. nests

75

Read the sentences below. Fill in each blank with the correct word. Remember a word can have more than one meaning.

scales   saw   safe   sale

1. The _____ is used to cut wood.

2. The shoes were cheaper in the _____.

3. They _____ a strange bird in a tree.

4. The bank keeps money in a _____.

5. Fish are covered with _____.

6. The _____ told them how heavy the box was.

7. Never play with matches. They are not _____.

8. That house on Barr Road is for _____.

D **Synonyms** are two or more words with similar meanings. Write each word from the column on the right next to its synonym in the column on the left.

1. hated _____ port

2. old _____ complain

3. harbor _____ groan

4. search _____ unusual

5. struggle _____ despised

6. shouted _____ unsafe

7. injure _____ hunt

8. grumble _____ laughed

9. inquire _____ fight

10. strange _____ thing

11. object _____ exclaimed

12. stones _____ ask

13. moan _____ antique

14. dangerous _____ hurt

15. giggled _____ pebbles

Below is a page from a dictionary. Use it to answer the following questions.

> **cab•i•net** (kăb′ ĭ nĕt) **1** *n* : a set of drawers **2** *n* : a piece of fur-
> niture with doors
> **cham•pi•on** (chăm′ pĭ ŭn) **1** *n* : one who defends weaker people
> **2** *n* : any person or thing that is best **3** *v* : to defend a person or
> idea
> **clue** (klōō) **1** *n* : something to help solve a problem **2**: a hint
> **coast** (kōst) **1** *n* : land at the edge of the sea **2** *v* : to slide down-
> hill on snow or ice
> **cob•bler** (kŏb′ ler) **1** *n* : a mender of shoes **2** *n* : a fruit pie made
> with a thick crust
> **cure** (kūr) **1** *n* : a way of healing a sick person **2** *v* : to make
> someone healthy again

1. How many meanings are given for the word *cabinet*?_____

2. How many syllables are in the word *champion*? _____

3. Which words have only one syllable each?_____

4. What is a kind of dessert? _____

5. Who is a person who tries to help people in need? _____

6. What are the correct guide words for this page? _____

7. Write all the entry words found on this dictionary page.

   _____

   _____

8. Which meaning of the word *cobbler* is used in this sentence:

   The cobbler bought some leather.

   _____

9. Which meaning of the word *coast* is used in this sentence:

   We watched the people coast on the bobsled.

   _____

10. Which meaning of the word *coast* is a noun?

   _____

11. Is *cure* used as a noun or a verb in this sentence:

   Veternarians can cure animal diseases.

   _____

We snakes do not have hands. Feet and eyelids are also among our missing parts. How would you like it if you could never close your eyes? The body parts we do have help us live in the animal world. See our long, slender, slinky shapes! We have a head, two eyes, a mouth, a forked tongue, and colorful scales. The scales on our stomachs help us crawl fast. The forked tongue helps us smell things. We breathe air with our lungs. Oh, yes, I almost forgot my fangs. They are as sharp as thorns and poisonous. They shoot venom into enemies that try to harm me. However, most snakes are not harmful!

Snakes are cold-blooded. This means that the temperature of our bodies is the same as the temperature of the air or water around us. If it is hot outdoors, we have high temperatures. If it is cold outdoors, we have low temperatures. In the winter, we must hibernate to keep from freezing.

We swallow our food whole. The prey we swallow is much larger than we are. Our mouths open very wide. Our jaws spread apart. Then gulp, the food is down! Look at my snake friend on page 79. He has just swallowed a large animal, and you can see the bulges in his body.

If all snakes liked the same food, there would not be enough food for all of us. Because of this, some of us eat

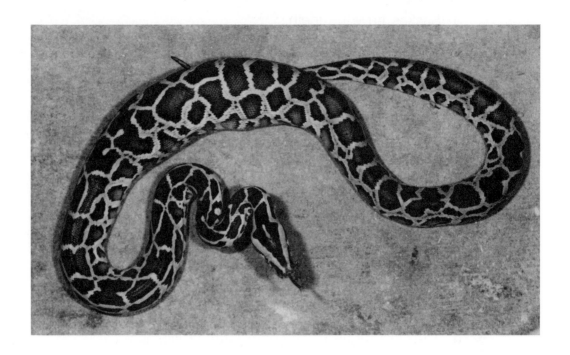

only eggs. Some snakes dine only on snails. Others enjoy meals of birds, rats, frogs, toads, or insects. I hate to mention this, but some of us are *cannibals*. A cannibal is one that eats its own kind. Some snakes eat other snakes.

We have many enemies. Human beings are the worst. They kill us for food and for our skin. Shoes, pocketbooks, wallets, belts, and jackets are made out of our beautiful, scaly hides. Scientists have learned to make medicine from our venom, too. Larger birds swoop down out of the sky to grab us for lunch. Wild pigs trample on smaller snakes and then eat them. Cobras and king snakes enjoy making meals out of smaller snakes, too.

Have these facts made you more interested in snakes? Watch for us all around you. Some of us are found in ponds and streams. Others may be seen on land and in gardens, woods, pastures, and trees. Most of us prefer damp, warm places such as swamps and jungles where we can be left alone.

Underline the correct answer for each question.

1. Which one of these sentences is untrue?

   a. Snakes have no teeth.

   b. Snakes close their eyes to sleep.

   c. Some snakes eat birds and toads.

   d. Some snakes have poisonous fangs.

2. In which of these do all the words describe snakes?

   a. jaws, forked tongue, eyelids

   b. fangs, scales, nails, forked tongue

   c. eyes, bodies, scales, toes

   d. scales, mouth, fangs, forked tongue

3. Why do some snakes avoid other snakes?

   a. They are afraid of being teased.

   b. They are afraid of being eaten.

   c. They are afraid of humans.

   d. They are afraid of getting a strange sickness.

4. What does *cold-blooded* mean?

   a. The animal is always cold.

   b. The blood has been kept on ice.

   c. The animal dies because it has no blood in its body.

   d. The body is the same temperature as the air or water around it.

5. Which sentence is true?

   a. When the air is hot, the snake is cold.

   b. Snakes have six tiny legs.

   c. Snakes use lungs to breathe.

   d. Snakes have gills for breathing.

6. In which of these do all the words describe foods for snakes?

   a. birds, dinosaurs, eggs

   b. fangs, nails, scales

   c. rats, insects, birds

   d. toads, other snakes, venom

7. How do snakes help people?

   a. They kill harmful insects and rats.

   b. They eat farmers' crops.

   c. Their bodies clean the ground as they slide along.

   d. They guard the homes of people.

8. What is the best title for this story?

   a. The Farmers' Best Friend

   b. Fear of Snakes

   c. How Snakes Protect Themselves

   d. Facts About Snakes

9. Why will we never see snakes with closed eyes?

   a. Snakes have no eyelids.

   b. They have only one eyelid.

   c. Their eyelids are very heavy.

   d. Snakes must watch for danger at all times.

10. How do snakes eat their prey?

    a. They chew it well.

    b. They trample it.

    c. They swallow it whole.

    d. They cook it first.

B Write the missing words to complete these sentences. Find the correct words in the snake basket. The first letter of each word is given.

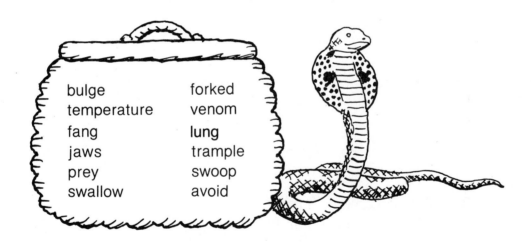

bulge	forked
temperature	venom
fang	**lung**
jaws	trample
prey	swoop
swallow	avoid

Slithering Sam is a very handsome cobra. When he speaks, he never finishes his sentences.

1. Sam says, "This story will bring tears to your eyes. I broke my

   f _____ by trying to gulp down a small wild pig. I struck, but I missed!

   It got to me first and began to t _____ on my face. Its

   hoof hit my f _____."

2. "I haven't gone to Dr. Pullem, our family dentist, yet because we were struck with a sudden heat wave. Because I am cold-blooded, my

   t _____ was so high that my stomach scales were burning as I crawled along the hot ground."

3. "I've got to be very careful sliding to Dr. Pullem's office. I don't have any

   v _____ in my broken f _____."

4. "There's a big, fat, bald eagle up in the rocks near Dr. Pullem's place. She's just waiting for poor, helpless me to come by. She'll

   s _____ down out of the sky and try to grab me."

5. Sam groans, "Oh! My f _____ tongue is being cut to

   ribbons by the sharp edge of that broken f _____."

6. Again Sam is complaining. "My stomach is flat, I can't swallow any

   p _____. How I would love to swallow a nice rat and see a big,

   round, b _____ in my slender body again."

7. "I'm going to take a deep breath of air in my l _____. Then with your kind help, I'll go to Dr. Pullem."

8. "Soon I will be able to s _____ a whole rat or a bird again!"

9. "Please come with me," begs Sam. "Maybe we can a _____

   that nasty eagle. I would hate to be the p _____ of a bird, of all things!"

10. "I can hardly wait to open my j _____ wide. Then I can start

    catching my p _____ once more!"

Our story had many important facts about snakes. To help remember them, we can make an **outline**. An outline has a special form:

> ★ Each outline should have a title that tells what the whole story is about.
> ★ Each outline must have the main topics or main ideas in the story. These are written with Roman numerals.
> ★ Under each main topic or main idea are details that tell more about the main topic. These are written with a capital letter in front of each detail.

Now look back at the story about snakes. The story has six paragraphs. Each paragraph has a main topic. From the Topic Box choose the main topic of paragraphs 1, 3, 4, 5, and 6. Skip paragraph 2. Write each main topic beside a Roman numeral.

Topic Box

How a snake eats
Enemies of snakes
Where snakes are found
What a snake eats
Body parts of snakes

Facts About Snakes

I. _____

   A. _____

   B. _____

   C. _____

   D. _____

   E. _____

III. _____

   A. _____

   B. _____

   C. _____

IV. _____

    A. _____

    B. _____

    C. _____

    D. _____

    E. _____

V. _____

    A. _____

    B. _____

    C. _____

    D. _____

VI. _____

    A. _____

    B. _____

    C. _____

    D. _____

    E. _____

    F. _____

Now look at the Detail Box. Find details for each main topic. Write them next to the capital letters under each main topic in the outline.

Detail Box

Gardens	Jaws that spread wide	Ponds
Rats	Woods	Scales
No eyelids or feet	Human beings	Large birds
Eggs	Bulges in body	Pigs
Jungles	Cold-blooded	Other snakes
Fangs	Toads	Eyelashes
Swallows prey whole	Swamps	Forked tongues
Lungs	Insects	Streams

D Read the facts below carefully. Then follow the directions to make an outline.

Fleas are dangerous, troublesome insects. They spread diseases from one animal to another. They carry sicknesses to human beings, too. They make animals and people uncomfortable.

The tiny body of the flea is difficult to see. It is flat, short, and pale. Fleas have no wings. Their long, strong hind legs make them good jumpers. They have a long, sharp, sucking beak on the head.

Fleas are found in many places. They may be hidden in the fur of rats, rabbits, cats, and dogs. They can be found in the feathers of pigeons, chickens, and ducks. In places where animals sleep, fleas are found in rugs, furniture, grass, dust, and cracks in the floor.

All fleas eat the same food. They use their sharp beaks to make a hole in the skins of people and animals. Then they suck the blood of their prey. Blood is the only food eaten by fleas.

Now put the information in a shorter form by outlining it. Choose the main topic for each paragraph from the Topic Box. Put each main topic by a Roman numeral. Be sure to put a title on your outline.

┌─────────────── **Topic Box** ───────────────┐

How fleas eat   Why fleas are dangerous
Where fleas live   What fleas look like

└───┘

_____

I. _____

   A. _____

   B. _____

   C. _____

II. _____

    A. _____

    B. _____

    C. _____

    D. _____

III. _____

    A. _____

    B. _____

    C. _____

    D. _____

    E. _____

IV. _____

    A. _____

    B. _____

Now look at the Detail Box. Find details for each main topic. Write the details next to the capital letters under each main topic.

Detail Box

No wings

Cracks in floors

Suck blood of prey

On animals' furs

Long, sharp, sucking beak

Spread diseases to humans

Spread diseases to animals

Make people and animals uncomfortable

Strong hind legs for jumping

Flat, short, pale

Places animals sleep

Make hole in skin of prey

In birds' feathers

Rugs and carpets

Pearls

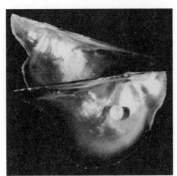

A pearl begins its life as a speck of sand or as a very small sea animal. Either of these can be swept into an oyster's shell. The oyster cannot get rid of this unwelcome visitor. The gritty sand or the biting sea animal hurts the oyster.

To protect itself, the oyster begins to cover the object with a layer of pearly material. After the object is completely covered, the oyster forms another layer over the first layer. It builds layer on top of layer until there is a round, shiny pearl inside the oyster shell.

Divers swim through cold ocean water to reach the oyster beds. Then they bring the oyster shells to the surface. After the oysters are washed, the shells are opened. The pearls are then removed.

The best pearls are used for necklaces. They are sold as jewelry.

Peanuts

This is a peanut plant. One day yellow flower buds on it open at sunrise. By noon, the blossoms are already dead. The bottom of each flower begins to grow, forming a *peg*. This peg is really a stem.

The stem or peg grows and begins to hang down to the ground. Then the peg pushes itself into the earth. The top of the peg has a little seed inside. As the stem goes deeper in the ground, the seed in the tip swells. It gets larger and larger until it becomes a peanut. Every flower grows into a peg. Every peg turns into a peanut.

The peanuts are picked by pulling the whole plant out of the earth. After the plant dries, the peanuts are removed.

Butterflies

The female butterfly always lays her eggs on leaves. She picks the kind of leaves the larvae will feed on. Not all butterfly larvae eat the same kinds of plants. In a few days, the eggs begin to hatch. The larvae come out. Butterfly larvae are known as *caterpillars*.

The caterpillars are greedy little creatures. They eat leaves until they are fat, round, and ready to burst. They become too large for their skins and shed them four or five times. Still, they keep eating.

After a caterpillar gets its fifth skin, it begins to spin a silk thread and fastens itself to a twig or leaf.

Once it is tied tightly, the caterpillar spins a silky thread all around its body. When it is completely covered, it is inside a cocoon. This is the pupa. The pupa inside the cocoon changes its appearance. When the cocoon bursts open, a weak and wet butterfly comes out. Slowly, it fans its wings, dries out, gets strong, and flies away. It is hard to believe that the butterfly was once a crawling caterpillar and an ugly pupa.

Pens

In ancient Rome, people used a pointed piece of bone or metal to write words on thin, waxed boards. Later, people wrote with hollow reeds. Hollow reeds are tall, stiff, plant stems. People wrote on pieces of parchment (animal skins). Ink was placed inside the hollow stem to make marks when the reed was pushed down on the parchment.

A few hundred years later, someone discovered that the long wing feathers of a swan or a goose made good pens. The end of the feather was sharpened into a point. These pens were called *quills*. Quills were used for many years.

To write on paper, it was necessary to add steel tips to the quills. In 1884, the first fountain pen was invented. These pens were filled with ink and wrote until the ink was gone. Then the pen could be filled again.

Fountain pens were mainly used until 1944. Ball-point pens were invented then. You probably write with a ball-point pen. In 1951, felt-tipped marker pens were first made.

A The following questions are about the four articles. You might need to look back and reread, or skim for information. Underline each correct answer.

1. Where are pearls found?

   a. in mines   b. in the desert   c. on trees   d. in the ocean

2. Something is wrong with this picture. What is it?

   a. The leaves are the wrong shape.

   b. The roots should be near the top.

   c. The peanuts are in the wrong place.

   d. The stem is in the wrong place.

3. On what did ancient Romans write at first?

   a. waxed boards   b. animal skins

   c. paper   d. parchment

4. What is a caterpillar?

   a. the egg   b. the pupa

   c. the larva   d. the adult

5. What is parchment?

   a. reeds or hollow stems   b. a sharp piece of bone

   c. a quill pen   d. animal skins to write on

6. Which sentence is *not* true?

    a. Caterpillars are greedy.

    b. The female butterfly lays eggs.

    c. Pearls are found in the shells of oysters.

    d. A caterpillar will eat any leaf.

7. Where are the eggs of butterflies laid?

    a. in flowers   b. under the ground

    c. on leaves   d. in the hive

8. How are pearls started?

    a. with some eggs laid by the oyster   b. with a speck of sand

    c. with layers of sand   d. with layers of skin

9. Why could fountain pens be used for a long time?

    a. The ink got used up.   b. They were made of bone.

    c. They could be refilled.   d. none of these

10. George Washington used a quill pen. With what was he writing?

    a. a cat tail

    b. a goose feather

    c. a large reed

    d. a ball-point pen

11. What hatches from butterflies' eggs?

    a. pupae   b. cocoons

    c. larvae   d. honeycombs

12. What must be done to find pearls?

    a. gather oysters from the hives

    b. dive into deep water to get oysters

    c. wait until the pupa bursts open

    d. gather cocoons from the ocean bottom

13. How are all these stories alike?

    a. Each story is about the lives of animals.

    b. Each story tells about the work of famous scientists and inventors.

    c. Each story tells how useful things were invented.

    d. Each story shows the order in which something happens.

Choose the correct word from the box for each picture. Write it under the picture.

pearls	board	caterpillar
plunge	parchment	ink
fountain pen	oyster	cocoon
peanut	ball-point pen	quill

1. _____ 2. _____ 3. _____

4. _____ 5. _____ 6. _____

7. _____ 8. _____ 9. _____

C Write the correct word to complete each sentence.

1. The larva of the _____ is called a caterpillar.

   ant   butterfly   pearl

2. The caterpillar changes into a _____.

   egg   quill   pupa

3. The peanut flower has a short _____.

   pearl   life   root

4. The covering around the pupa is called a _____.

   larva   pupa   cocoon

5. When the peanut flower dies, a small _____ begins to grow.

   peg   pig   egg

6. An adult butterfly comes out of the _____.

   cocoon   reed   parchment

7. Writing paper made from animal skins is called _____.

   larva   parchment   honeycomb

8. The peg becomes the _____.

   pupa   pearl   peanut

9. Peanuts grow _____.

   on the stems above the ground
   on the stems under the ground
   on the leaves over the stems

10. The caterpillar sheds its _____.

    peg   cocoon   skin

11. A quill may be a swan's _____.

    quilt   father   feather

12. An unwelcome visitor to the oyster in its shell may be a

    _____.

    sea animal   cocoon   peg

13. Another unwelcome visitor inside the oyster shell could be a

    _____.

    speck of sand   oyster pupa   bird's feather

D Read the information below. Then answer the questions by writing the letter of the correct answer next to the questions.

Everything's in Order

All things move in order from one stage to another. You have grown from a tiny infant to the young person you are now. You will go through more orderly stages until you are an adult. Now see what you can remember about the stages of peanuts, butterflies, pens, and pearls.

If you have forgotten, look back and skim the articles.

1. a. the fountain pen
   b. quills with sharpened points
   c. hollow reeds filled with ink
   d. the felt-tipped marker

   Which comes first? _____

   Which comes second? _____

   Which comes third? _____

   Which comes last? _____

2. a. The caterpillar gets too fat for its skin.
   b. It spins a cocoon all around itself.
   c. The eggs hatch.
   d. The greedy caterpillar stuffs itself.
   e. It gets a new skin.
   f. It spins a thread and fastens itself to a twig.

   Which comes first? _____

   Which comes second? _____

   Which comes third? _____

   Which comes fourth? _____

   Which comes fifth? _____

   Which comes sixth? _____

1. When do peanut flowers die?
   a. soon after sunset
   b. before noon
   c. in the morning
   d. just before midnight

2. When do the pegs push into the ground?
   a. before the buds open
   b. after the pegs grow downward
   c. while the flowers are blooming
   d. after the flower blossoms die

3. When should the peanuts be picked?
   a. before the flower bud opens
   b. after the plant is taken out of the ground
   c. after the plant and the peanuts have dried
   d. before the leaves grow

4. When did people start to write on paper?
   a. after they used parchment
   b. before fountain pens were invented
   c. before they used parchment
   d. after ball-point pens were invented

5. When were steel tips put on quill pens?
   a. before sharpened bones were used
   b. after felt-tipped pens were invented
   c. when writing paper was used by many people
   d. before fountain pens were invented

6. When do the caterpillars shed their skin?
   a. after eating a lot and getting very fat
   b. after hatching out of the eggs
   c. after going through the pupa stage
   d. while they are butterflies

F Here are the eight stages in a butterfly's life. Write them in order. The first one is done for you.

Stages of a Butterfly

The caterpillar spins a cocoon.
The caterpillar sheds its skin.
The adult butterfly flies away.
The larva hatches from an egg.
The butterfly bursts out of its cocoon.
The pupa hangs quietly in the cocoon.
The greedy caterpillar eats and eats.
The butterfly dries out.

1. The female butterfly lays eggs. _____

_____

2. _____

_____

3. _____

_____

4. _____

_____

5. _____

_____

6. _____

_____

7. _____

_____

8. _____

_____

9. _____

_____

Dennis Dolphin took a deep breath of salty air. Arching his back, he dived into the ocean.

He was a few months past his first birthday and had just begun to live on his own.

"I think that today I will explore closer to the bottom," thought Dennis. "Maybe I will find a new kind of fish to eat."

He swam lower and bumped into a school of mackerels. But they were not what he wanted. Dennis kept swimming.

Among some purple rocks, he saw a flash of green. Then out came a long, skinny tentacle which neatly captured a passing crab. A strange shape with eight tentacles oozed out of the rocks to swallow the crab.

Few animals are more curious than dolphins. Dennis hurried to investigate this sea creature. He poked his bottle-shaped nose at it.

Though Dennis did not realize it, he was staring at an octopus. Her name was Amy. Like all of her kind, she wanted to be left alone. Her green eyes examined the dolphin's big nose and huge grin.

"Ugh!" hissed Amy. "I don't care for company. Take that toothy smile of yours and disappear, fish!"

"I'm not a fish!" exclaimed Dennis. "I'm a mammal. I have to breathe air."

"So?" sneered Amy. "I'm not a fish either. But I don't swim around flashing all those big teeth at strangers."

"That grin is what makes us so lovable," boasted Dennis.

"To me you look like a silly clown," said Amy coldly.

"That's just what everyone calls us! Sea clowns!" laughed Dennis. "Humans think we're smart and beautiful!"

Amy and Dennis enjoyed each other's company. Their friendship grew. For several weeks they traveled together—dining, chatting, and having fun.

Dennis knew more about the outside world than Amy did. Every fifteen minutes he had to rise to the surface of the ocean to breathe. Dennis told Amy about the things he saw.

When curious dolphins hear a new sound, they must swim over to investigate. One evening, they heard the noise of some engines. Like all dolphins, Dennis could swim very quickly. He dashed over and saw a big ship.

Amy was left behind. She did not trust ships. They often had big nets to catch fish. Sometimes octopuses and even dolphins were trapped with the fish.

"Wait, Dennis!" she yelled.

It was too late. A school of huge tuna fish were passing by. Down came a large net. It covered all the tunas and poor Dennis.

Amy looked on in shock as Dennis wildly threw himself against the net. He tried to get free again and again. But the strands were too strong.

"I must be out of here in eight minutes!" cried Dennis. "I need to go up to breathe air."

"When the fishers raise the nets, they will free you," suggested Amy. "You don't look like a tasty snack."

The dolphin said sadly, "They may not pull in the net until tomorrow."

Amy thought fast. Suddenly her tentacles started to tear at the net. They ripped and tore until an opening appeared. Soon it was large enough for Dennis to squeeze through. Out he burst! Away he swam to the top of the ocean.

Then Amy skillfully began to repair the torn edges. With her eight tentacles, she could make tight knots. The net was stronger than before.

"The fishers now can catch some more fish," said Amy.

Dennis smiled, "Thank you, Amy. You saved my life!"

Amy said softly, "That's what friends are for, Dennis."

A Underline the correct answer to each question.

1. Where did Dennis Dolphin find Amy Octopus?
   a. in a group of oysters
   b. in a fishing net
   c. at the bottom of a lake
   d. in the crack of some rocks

2. What was this story mainly about?
   a. two friends fighting
   b. the life of an octopus in the ocean
   c. how tuna fish are caught
   d. friends helping one another

3. How often did Dennis need to breathe air?
   a. three times a day
   b. about every fifteen minutes
   c. once every two hours
   d. The story does not say.

4. Why did Dennis leave Amy as soon as he was freed?

    a. He blamed Amy for his getting caught.

    b. He needed to breathe.

    c. He was racing a tuna.

    d. He wanted to get even with the fishermen.

5. Which of the following is a fish?

    a. mackerel   b. octopus

    c. dolphin   d. mammal

6. Why was Dennis captured?

    a. He was trying to catch a tuna for Amy to eat.

    b. He was curious about a sound.

    c. He was trying to free Amy from the net.

    d. He wanted to get on the ship.

7. How did Dennis escape from the net?

    a. Amy tore the strands.

    b. The fishers let him go.

    c. He chewed on the net.

    d. Dennis threw himself against the net until it broke.

8. What were Amy's best tools?

    a. crab shells   b. sharp claws

    c. long tentacles   d. sharp teeth

9. When did Amy repair the net?

    a. before Dennis escaped

    b. before she met Dennis

    c. while Dennis was in the net

    d. after Dennis got out

10. How did Amy fix the net?

    a. by ripping and tearing

    b. by throwing away strands

    c. by tying knots in the strands

    d. by sewing strands together

11. Why do you think people call dolphins "sea clowns"?

    a. They are mammals who need air.

    b. They do tricks and seem to smile.

    c. They swim backward.

    d. They look like circus clowns.

Write the correct word from the list below to complete each sentence.

mackerel	huge	boast
clever	grin	disappeared
dolphin	mammal	strand
tuna	examine	investigate

1. Someone who is smart and witty is called _____.

2. A smiling mammal that lives in the ocean is the _____.

3. To look at closely is to _____.

4. Two kinds of fish are the _____ and the

   _____.

5. To draw back the lips and show the teeth is to _____.

6. Something that is never seen again has _____.

7. To brag about oneself is to _____.

8. A thing that is very large is _____.

9. A string is a _____.

 To draw a **conclusion**, you must have enough information. Sometimes people draw conclusions without knowing all the details. Then their conclusions can be wrong. Read the information below. Then draw a sensible conclusion. Underline the correct conclusion.

1. Dolphins need air to breathe. They must come to the top of the water often. We can say that dolphins mostly stay

   a. at the bottom of the sea.

   b. near the surface.

   c. on land.

2. Far beneath the surface of the ocean, everything is different. It is always very cold and very dark there. The creatures that live there are strange-looking. Some of them have their own lights to see by. We can say that

   a. the sun only shines a few hours a day deep in the ocean.

   b. the sunlight is very weak at the ocean bottom.

   c. the sunlight never reaches the ocean bottom.

3. If you could dive two miles down in the ocean, you would find darkness. With a lantern, you would be able to see water, rocks, strange fish, and tiny sea animals. You would see no living plants. We can say that

   a. the fish have eaten all the plants.

   b. some plants grow best in the darkness.

   c. plants cannot live there without light.

4. When Dennis was caught in the net, Amy had to rescue him. If she had not freed him, he would not have reached the surface to breathe air. What would have happened to Dennis in the net? We can say that

   a. he would have gotten very sick.

   b. he would have died.

   c. he would have become thin.

5. All mammals must breathe air. Mammals take air into their lungs. Horses, lions, monkeys, and humans have lungs. Fish are not mammals because they have no lungs. They have gills to take in oxygen from the water. Fish die when taken from the water into the air. We can say that

   a. dolphins have gills.

   b. dolphins have lungs.

   c. fish have lungs.

6. Fish have heads, tails, fins, gills, mouths, and noses. They have eyes, but no eyelids. We can say that fish

   a. sleep with their eyes closed.

   b. sleep with their eyes half-shut.

   c. sleep with their eyes open.

7. Fish are cold-blooded. They are the same temperature as the water around them. If the water is cold, the temperatures of the fish are low. We can say that if the temperatures of the fish are high,

   a. the water is cold.   b. the water is warm.   c. the fish have a fever.

8. All fish live in water, but not all animals in the water are fish. Fish must have fins and gills. Jellyfish and starfish do not have fins. So we can say

   a. that they are not fish.

   b. that they are fish.

   c. that they are mammals.

9. Baby dolphins learn from their mothers. They must stay close to their mothers for twelve months. Dennis is now on his own. We can say that

   a. Dennis has not left his mother yet.

   b. Dennis is under a year old.

   c. Dennis is more than a year old.

D Sometimes we cannot draw sensible conclusions from our reading. Not enough information is given to us. Reread the story of Dennis Dolphin and Amy Octopus. Then read each sentence below. Each statement might be true or false, or there might not be enough details in the story for you to decide. Write the letter of the correct conclusion for each sentence.

T—True
F—False
N—Not enough information was given

_____ 1. Mackerels swim in large groups.

_____ 2. Tuna fish are caught in nets.

_____ 3. Dolphins swim eighty miles an hour.

_____ 4. Tuna fishers clean the tuna on board their fishing boats.

_____ 5. Tunas are tiny fish.

_____ 6. Dolphins are friendly and curious.

_____ 7. The fishers ate dolphins.

_____ 8. Octopuses must come to the surface to breathe.

_____ 9. Dolphins sometimes get caught in fishing nets.

E Read the information below. Then write a sensible conclusion for each set of statements.

1. a. All dolphins are mammals.
   b. Mammals must breathe air.

   c. _____

2. a. All fish have fins and gills.
   b. Amy does not have fins.

   c. _____

3. a. Octopuses must breathe underwater.
   b. Mammals must breathe above water.

   c. _____

The Swallowtail Butterfly

A tiger swallowtail butterfly has a little different life than other butterflies. The larva comes out of an egg laid on a green leaf. At that time it does not look like the usual caterpillar. It looks like a piece of black, brown, and white dirt. This is lucky for the larva. Birds do not look at it. The larva chews on leaves and gets fat.

Twice the larvae shed their old skins. Each time the new skin is greener. The third new skin makes them look just like a green caterpillar. But again they try to fool the birds that would eat them. The green caterpillar has two spots on its head. These black, yellow, and white spots look like a snake's eyes. Birds that do not eat snakes do not bother the larva. It eats, gets fat, and grows.

Soon the caterpillar or larva spins a silky thread. With the thread it fastens itself to a tree. Then the larva spins and covers its entire body with a cocoon. The pupa, or cocoon, looks just like a piece of tree bark. It hangs on a twig and is hard to see.

When the adult butterfly bursts out of the cocoon, it is changed in color. It is a beautiful black and yellow tiger swallowtail. Some females are black and blue instead of yellow. They look just like another kind of butterfly that birds do not like to eat. Again the birds are fooled. They do not eat the black tiger swallowtails, which would taste good.

A Underline the correct answer to each question.

1. When does the pupa stage come?
   a. after the larva stage
   b. before the larva stage
   c. before the egg stage

2. When does the butterfly look like a piece of dirt?
   a. during the pupa stage
   b. when it is in the egg
   c. during the larva stage

3. When does the caterpillar attach itself to a tree?
   a. after it spins a cocoon
   b. when it is an adult
   c. before it spins a cocoon

4. When is the tiger swallowtail butterfly a green caterpillar?
   a. as soon as it hatches out of the egg
   b. before it looks like a piece of dirt
   c. after it looks like a piece of dirt

5. What is the pupa stage?
   a. the larva stage
   b. the egg stage
   c. the cocoon stage

6. When does the larva get a new skin?
   a. after the caterpillar eats a lot
   b. after the pupa eats a lot
   c. before the larva eats anything

7. When do tiger swallowtails fool the birds?
   a. only in the adult stage
   b. in the larva, pupa, and adult stages
   c. only when it looks like a piece of dirt

8. When do butterflies have snake-eye spots?
   a. when they are larvae
   b. when they are pupae
   c. when they are eggs

Reread the story of the tiger swallowtail butterfly. It tells us some information about butterflies. But it does not tell everything. Here are some questions. You can answer some of them. Others you were not given enough information to answer. Write the words **not enough information** below each question for which you were not given enough information. Answer the questions for which you were given information.

1. How many kinds of butterflies are there in the United States?

   _____

2. What color are tiger swallowtail butterflies usually?

   _____

3. What is the larva stage of the butterfly called?

   _____

4. Name one animal that eats butterflies.

   _____

5. Are there fewer butterflies in the world today than there were 100 years ago?

   _____

6. What is the pupa stage of a butterfly called?

   _____

7. How are butterflies like moths?

   _____

8. Do butterflies have ears?

   _____

9. How long does it take butterfly eggs to hatch?

   _____

10. Where are cocoons found?

   _____

Read about baby spiders. Then number the pictures to show the order in which these things happen.

First, the female spider spins a thin silk saucer. She lays many eggs on it. To protect the eggs, she builds a silk cocoon all around them. Inside the cocoon the babies hatch from the eggs, but they do not look like spiders yet. They shed their skins inside the crowded nest. When they look like tiny adults, they must tear a hole in the strong silk. One at a time, they struggle out of the cocoon. Spinning a soft silk thread lets them drift away in different directions to begin their own webs to trap food.

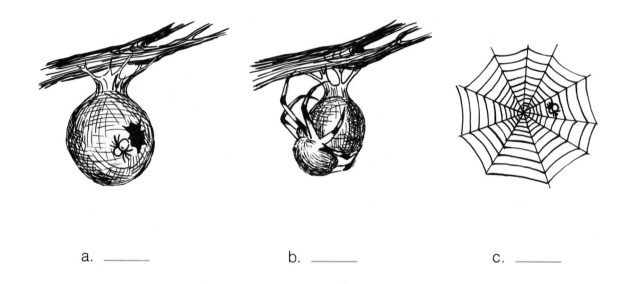

a. _____   b. _____   c. _____

d. _____   e. _____

D How much do you remember? Write the names of three objects on the pearl necklace. Write the names of six mammals on the elephant. Write six verbs or action words on the shark.

Word Box

caught	dolphins	laid
quill	parchment	investigate
humans	spins	fountain pen
burst	dogs	horses
cows	flies	cats

Read the following article about the onager. Then write the correct details below. Write a title for the outline.

Onager is the name of an animal in the horse family. It is wild and travels in a herd. The onager looks very much like a donkey. In the summer it is dark brown, but in the winter its fur coat turns to yellowish-brown. It has a black stripe down its back. The onager has a mane. At the end of its tail is a tuft of hair.

Herds of onagers can be found on the hot, dry grasslands of central Asia. They are very fast runners. This protects them from their enemies.

I.   What the onager looks like

    A. _____

    B. _____

    C. _____

    D. _____

II. How the onager protects itself

    A. _____

    B. _____

    C. _____

III. Where onagers are found

    A. _____

    B. _____

    C. _____

    D. _____